A kink's per A-Z guide to BDSM

by
alister mcleod

Forward by Mistress D

Welcome to the world of the male slave.

Since "50 Shades of Grey" everyone wants to know about domination and submission and there are lots of tales of submissive girls and Dominant men out there.

But many women are dominant not submissive and men can be submissive too.

This book describes real life; the secret things a Mistress and Her slave get up to. My slave wrote it with my support and supervision to provide a guide to the most common BDSM activities including the risks involved. But it also explains some of the deep psychological issues involved as well for True Submission comes from the inside and he describes this well.

The guide is explicit and not for the faint hearted. There is lots of detail on all the activities which shows how they work out in practice, and he gives examples of what has worked out with Me as his Mistress and owner and him as my slave.

If you are a man who is interested in submission and male slavery you must read this; it shows you the way to develop your submissive side. A woman will see in this book some ideas on how to train a slave of your own.

Mistress D...2013

Introduction to the kink's personal A to Z guide for the male slave

There is a lot of information available from books and the internet about the whole world of BDSM. Some of it is true but a lot of the accounts of what happens are made up fiction and fantasies that people would like to experience but have no basis in fact. This makes it difficult to know what to believe.

This guide is different. It is organised as and A to Z guide but it is also a personal account written by one who is a man and a slave. my Mistress who has been training me for years and doing all sorts of things with and to me decided that She wanted me to write a guide based on our knowledge and experience. So it is a personal A to Z guide.

The topics chosen are those that Mistress has identified herself and those suggested by her friends. She decided the topics and i wrote the content which She then checked for accuracy and to make sure that i had not missed anything out.

They cover the whole world of being a male slave, all forms of bondage and many different types of bondage equipment that She has used over the years with details of the very many of the things that Mistress can do to Her slaves.

It also discusses issues of control where Mistress is in control of a slave and uses Her power to decide what is to happen. Mistress also decides what services She wants from Her slaves.

A major part of being a slave is not just the physical control that Mistress wields but the psychological dominance and control over a slave. Mistress dominates and Her slaves consent fully to submit and obey Her. Submission and obedience are essential and failure may lead to punishment. Mistress accepts freely the power given to her by Her slaves and uses it fully.

Although pain is part of the picture all the other senses can be subverted and overwhelmed by what Mistress chooses to do, whether removing the sense of sight or hearing or enhancing touch or adding in heat, cold and vibration to the mix.

The correct place for a slave is to be on his knees or prostrate before his Mistress and to learn to enjoy submission and obedience.

Even though he may be bound, gagged and blindfolded a slave is free. He is "free" from the limitations of "normal" life to develop his obedience and submission. Over time this grows deeper and takes over areas of his mind until his bondage and slavery become an issue of psychological domination and power more than anything physical.

i have placed these topics within an A to Z framework but many areas are covered from different directions whilst coming from the same theme or interest. There are many different ways to secure a slave in bondage so there are a number of entries for bondage and separate ones for bondage equipment.

You can look for themes and the topics associated with them or just see what is there wherever you open the book.

But can you be certain that what is written here is not just fantasy and wishful thinking? i can only share with you what i am and how i got to my present position as a slave and ask you to take on trust that Mistress has put so much effort into both training me and checking what i have written to be certain that is correct.

i am sure that i have not covered everything in this A to Z guide and there are bound to be omissions which others might see to be important. What is important to Mistress and what She does to her slaves may not be exactly the same as others might do and emphasis will differ with different Mistresses and their slaves.

A slave's life is not always solely that of a slave full time because he might have a home life and a busy job and this affects what is possible. he might yearn to be tattooed with my Mistress's mark or slave registration number or to be formally branded as a slave but it is not practical. Mistress might prefer a slave completely without hair including on his head but it would not work out so well if he has a public or home life as well. However Brazilian waxing to remove hairs from more private areas has proved successful.

This personal A to Z guide covers most areas of life and activity for a slave and can provide knowledge for those who contemplate such a life of submission in their lives.

Mistress wanted it: i was ordered to write it; my task in life is to submit to Mistress and to obey; here is the result.

About the slave:

i am a man. To the outside world there is nothing unusual to see. i am of average height with greying hair and dress conservatively often in a suit and always with a tie. i tend to stand straight and occasionally will be seen to wince if i am sitting on a hard chair for too long in a meeting. i have a bad shoulder with wear and tear to the joint and my trips for "physiotherapy" for it may conceal attendance on Mistress. i have been both employed and run my own business and i travel on business from time to time. i have a family and a garden at home and can talk about work, the weather, or even occasionally the political situation. It all seems very mundane.

But underneath my outer clothing it is different for i am a slave. i wear a steel chastity device locked in place whenever i am out of the house and often have a butt plug deep inside me. i am in ankle chains and a steel collar with the collar hidden by my shirt and tie and the chains by my socks. i stand straight because i may be wearing a heavy leather corset covered by an elastane "spanx" vest and my lower parts are covered with elastane rich compression tights and pants. i am a slave and proud to be so though the outside world knows nothing of what is going on.

i have a Mistress who owns me and controls me. She decides what i wear under my outer clothing, my food for lunch, and my exercise regime at night. She decided i would wear a butt plug even in bed at night at home. i carry out the tasks She gives me, preparing material for a blog She publishes and writing this A to Z guide..

i have been a slave for over 14 years to a succession of Mistresses who have trained me. When i am able to be with Mistress i am placed in bondage and restriction, locked in a cage or cupboard or overnight in a tight bondage bag. i am expected to cope with nipple torment, CBD, larger butt plugs, dildos and given electric shocks. Mistress beats me, flogs me and whips me when She wants to.

i am in service in Her uniform carrying out cleaning and any other domestic task She desires. i provide personal services when She wants them including foot massage. But all the time i am constrained by the chastity device She purchased for me to wear and i live by Her rules. Then She has total control over me and it is such a wonderful experience and gives me such pleasure. But all the time, even when i am not with her She has a major effect on my mind. In my mind i am a slave 24/7, always waiting for the next email or text message, crushed by the corset and held in the chastity. It is the psychological chains that hold me. But She also protects me from myself. She helps keep me focussed so i can appear "normal" at home and at work and not let things slip. She controls the whole of my secret life.

Of course if i fail Her or disobey Her i am at risk of punishment and that is right. She sits in Judgement in all Her Power and Majesty and decides the sentence and i must bear it. That is how it should be.

So how did i end up like this?

It all probable goes back to my childhood when a girl in our neighbourhood used to terrorise and control the other children and tie them up and i found it exciting. As a young adult i had fantasies of being in the power of a Beautiful and Powerful Lady and being made to submit to Her and obey Her. That is what i always thought of and it formed the basis of all my fantasies.

After years of thinking about it and occasionally buying magazines i finally got up the courage to visit a Professional Mistress. i liked being tied up and all She did but i was confused and was not sure i really wanted this sort of thing or not. Still it was extremely exciting.

Over the years i visited Professional Dominant Mistresses no more than once a year or even less. i worked hard in business, settled down and had a family. But i always felt an unfulfilled desire to submit and obey and that something was missing in my life

Then i came across my first Mistress who taught me to enjoy bondage and that is was all about psychological domination as well as physical; Her power over me, power given by me, consented to freely and with definite boundaries set by contract. That was 14 years ago. That Mistress retired and passed me on to a friend and then in 2007 i came under the control of my present Mistress.

Mistress has such psychological dominance that i immediately wanted to be Her slave. She took me on and has worked to train me ever since. She has introduced me to so many forms of bondage and restraint and got me to spend long periods in isolation and sensory deprivation. She enjoys flogging and beating slaves and i have discovered that i like it too, especially as She is enjoying herself. She has trained me to provide domestic and personal services and has me writing a blog for Her and now this book.

Together we have moved towards introducing new restraint and training into the rest of my life. A couple of years ago She suddenly decided that i was no longer Her slave but was now Her property. This seemed so right and describes my state.

So now i have been ordered to write this personalised A to Z guide for male slaves incorporating some of my experiences. Of course some topics Mistress chose for me to write about are new to me and not something i had done before which is why i have now been introduced to the feelings of being crushed by a tight corset and to be Mistress's ashtray. i wonder what She will think of next.

Themes and interests

It is a highly subjective decision to allocate individual items to specific themes. It all depends upon the Mistress and Her slave and how they see things and the context. For some people being made to attend a beauty therapist for a Brazilian Wax treatment could be seen as a humiliation, and having all the hair removed would reduce their manhood and prepare them for feminization. Others like myself see it simply as yet another area of control mistress has over me and my life. She wants it done; i obey.

Similarly i enjoy being beaten and flogged; i like the sensations, i know Mistress is enjoying herself and it is a good feeling, but a severe caning is different and feels like the punishment it is.

So for any Mistress and any slave the categories will be different. They will choose the activities they like for enjoyment or those the slave does not like for punishment.
They may only do some things and others will not appeal to them. Both need to agree and consent is always the base of everything we do.

Areas of the body: all for Mistress to torment
    See:
Arse: all in the "impact" section, arse, butt plug, dildo, electrics, figging
Mouth: mouth, ashtray, gags, food control, urine
Nipples: nails, nipples, clamps, weights, jewels, shock collar
Cock and balls   CBT, chastity, shock collar, electrics, weights

Bondage: renders the slave helpless
    See:
Bondage, bondage at work, cuffs, chains, collar, gags, handcuffs, hoods, humbler, leg irons, leash, manacles, mummification, overnight sessions, pervertible, posture collar, predicament bondage, rope, suspension, training, torment and torture, weights, X position

Bondage equipment
    See:
Body bag, cage, cupboard, confinement in a car boot, dungeon, pressure, rack, spreader bar, straightjacket, stocks, weights, wheel, whipping bench

Electrics
    See:
Chastity devices, electrics, dildo, shock collar, violet wand, vibrator, zapped

Fetish: so many areas, so many fetishes
    See:
Ashtray, boots, breath control, chastity, feet, forced feminization, fetish, hair, Latex, leather, military, medical, rubber, shopping, sissy, tights, trampling

Humiliation: Difficult to define for there are some slaves who may find something humiliating whilst others would enjoy it. Some find it humiliating to be gagged and only able to drool.
    See:
Ashtray, Brazilian wax, butt plug, chastity, corsets, collar, forced feminization, gags, humiliation, leash, Sissy, spanx, tights, training,

Impact: hitting the slave
    See:
Arse, bastinado, caning, crop, flogging, kicking, nails, paddle, punishment, spanking, Switch, tawse, torment and torture, whip

Mistress is in control of the slave
    See:
bondage, bondage at work, branding, Brazilian wax, breath control, chastity, chastity devices, corsets, consent, contract, collar, exercise, food control, judgement, masturbation, overnight sessions, ownership, piercing, posture, pressure, remote control, sensory deprivation, sex, spanx, stress positions, tattoo, training, topping from the bottom, violation of orders, weights, work,

Psychology: working on the mind of the slave
    See:
Chastity, chastity contract, consent, domination, discipline, disorientation and darkness, female supremacy, female lead relationships, isolation, jewels, key holding, masturbation, overnight sessions, ownership, posture, power and power exchange, punishment, quiet, reality, safe and sane, safe word, secret life, submission, tattoo, temperament, time, training, uncertainty, vulnerable, whipping slave, YES Mistress.

Sensation: stimulation and restriction of the sensory inputs
    See:
Blindfold, candles, clamps, disorientation and darkness, gags, heating cream, hoods, isolation, ice, kidnapping, needles, pervertible, quiet, sensory deprivation, sensation and stimulation, violet wand, vibrators, wax, zapped, zipper.

Service: Mistress deserves to be served by Her slave.
    See:
Ashtray, Boots, Domestic service, feet, hair, Personal service, Financial servitude

Miscellaneous: might fit in many sections or none
     See:
Kidnapping, travel, water torture

How to use this book

This is not necessarily a book to read from front to back with each section one after another. If you have a particular interest look at the section above on themes and interests and it may guide you.

If you open the book at random and find something interesting the footnote to each section will point you to other sections of a similar content or interest.

If you have already started along the journey to submission and obedience in your life Your Mistress or owner may be the person who will want to use the book to guide you, or you could read sections together.

If you are still contemplating making a start on becoming a slave and learning what it might involve the book will give you pointers but only actual experience will tell you whether the reality will be right for you

Whoever you are whether a novice or more experienced there may be things here which you may never have thought about and want to try.

The book is here for everyone who has an interest in the life of a male slave to a powerful Mistress or who is thinking about trying it themselves.

Enjoy yourselves.

A note on Capitalisation

Very Important People are so important that their importance can be expressed by the use of Capital Letters when writing about them. When i write about Mistress or Her needs and desires and any other Women, Female Supremacy or Female Lead Relationships i use capitals.

A slave is naturally inferior to his Mistress and this can be expressed by his being considered as such in print. He is i not I; he is never He but he. Only Mistress requires a Capital letter and property and slaves only lower case without capitals.

So in this book i is always i, and Mistress is with a capital letter. This is how life should be and the text should reflect the Position and Power of the Mistress and submission to the lower case that of the lowly slave.

A is for ashtray

All parts of a slave belong to his Mistress, whether his backside for beating, his nipples for tormenting and his cock and balls. The mouth is an important part of that ownership.

Mistress may expect the slave to address Her in certain ways, to keep quiet unless allowed to speak, and to eat and drink what She decides. She can order the slave to his knees to eat and drink out of a dog bowl as the animal that he is. She may require him to wear a gag to keep him silent, especially if She is going to beat him severely and does not want him to make loud noises.

All of a slave is there to serve the Mistress, so if She likes to smoke then She will have need of an ashtray. This may be a problem if She is moving around and does not want to carry one with Her, or the ashtray is out of reach. This is one reason why a slave may be needed to act as an ashtray for his Mistress.

Some slaves may like it, and enjoy the taste of their Mistress's ash in their mouth. The slave may see this as a humiliation or degradation that helps them to focus on being a slave. Some slaves may not enjoy it but wish to find ways to serve Mistress in all ways possible. A few may not be able to cope and be sick. Slaves will need to practice to take Mistress's ash as She drops it into their mouth and swallow it.

It does not really matter if the slave enjoys it; what matters is what the Mistress thinks. She is in control and if She suggests that Her slave should serve in this way then many slaves will agree. There needs to be care, to make sure the ash does not spill, or is so hot as to burn, but it is a good opportunity for a slave to serve his Mistress

In my case i had not thought of it as a service that Mistress might wish until She was producing a list of issues for the male slave A to Z so i could be required to write notes on them for potential publication. She added it to the list so i realised it was something

She had thought about. It did not sound very nice, but then i have become used to Mistress requiring me to eat cat or dog food sometimes laced with chillies and fluff from the vacuum cleaner or even dusted with her cigarette ash so it was not so big a step.

Now i am used as Her ash tray when She decides, and must expect a mouth tasting of ash. She has already used me in this way and it was not as bad as i had feared. She wants it and it is another wonderful way to serve, so it is likely to continue. She decides, i consent, and so i am become an ash tray, no different from being Her footstool or any other type of furniture that She may decide She wants.

(See also, domination, humiliation, mouth, personal service, punishment, submission)

A is for arse

i take the term arse to apply to that part of the body which sticks out to the rear, skin covered mounds of muscle with a cleft in between leading down to the opening of the entry to the bowels. All parts of this should be under the control of the Mistress in every way.

The skin of the bottom is a favourite site for impact play with a variety of things used to hit the area. It is a perfect target for spanking with the hands, paddling, whipping and flogging, and the use of the cane. These can be applied either gently or with the full force of the Mistress's arm, leaving the backside tingling, red, or bruised or even with the skin broken. The sensation of being hit in this area can vary from the pleasant to a feeling of severe pain. Sometimes the slave may have difficulty sitting down afterwards for hours or even days.

It is important that anything that is done is done with the consent of both the Mistress and the slave. The slave needs to consent to what is done to him, but equally the Mistress does not want to be pressured into applying more force than She feels happy to deliver with the risk of damage to the slave. It all requires communication, and if it becomes too intense the use of some "safe-word" to get the Mistress to stop or change target. Sometimes a plea for mercy can mean just a change in target not stopping the torment.

All these methods to stimulate or punish a slave depend on the slave keeping the target still, so sometimes it is best to keep the slave still with some form of restraint.
But the buttocks can be stimulated in so many other ways as well. A soft rubbing may feel good, and the Mistress can use Her nails to trace out patterns on the bare backside. The substance of the buttocks can be grabbed and squeezed, and the stimulus can vary from mild to severe. It is one of the best sites to stimulate, for the

slave never knows what is coming next, particularly if he has been blindfolded or hooded. Ice can be applied or heating cream rubbed in or wax dripped onto the skin to stimulate further.

All of these are ways in which a Mistress can stimulate and have fun with a slave's buttocks. But the slave may also be expected to keep his backside in the state Mistress expects and to exercise so his buttocks are not flabby or soft but firm and full of muscle. Mistress may set the slave exercises to do every day to improve his muscle tone and the texture of the buttocks that belong to her. She may also wish to make the slave wear clothing to compress the buttocks so he has a feeling of being crushed at all times. This will remind him that he is Her slave. She may also want the area waxed to remove all hair.

(See also: Brazilian wax, caning, compressive clothing, crop, flogging, paddle, heating cream, ice, punishment, spanking, whipping)

Between the mounds of the buttocks lies the cleft leading to the anus. Slaves need to keep this clean and may be expected to have the area waxed to remove all hairs. This is the entrance to the anus area so it must be kept clean and ready for Mistress and as She wishes it presented.

The anus is the opening into the bowels, and this is where the Mistress can penetrate deep into Her slave. There are always risks to any anal activity, of bleeding, of infection and of damage that could leave the slave incontinent. So there must always be care. This is a total invasion of the private parts, and to allow your Mistress access here is to allow Her total power over you as a slave. The first time a slave is penetrated here he knows he is now there to be used as the plaything of Mistress and She shows Her power over him by taking control of this area.

In sessions there are so many things that can be inserted to give the slave pleasure or torment and for the Mistress to enjoy using. There are so many toys that it is difficult to know where to begin. It is important to use items that will not slip inside and be stuck there so they need to have a base to prevent this if they are going to be left in place. There are butt plugs, dildos and strap on devices of all shapes and sizes and the slave must expect to be tried with a variety of such items to find out which ones work on him and which ones the Mistress enjoys the most and which give the Mistress the greatest pleasure when She uses them. Some have an external hook which can be attached to a bondage harness or to somewhere to secure a slave in the position the Mistress desires. Freshly peeled ginger inserted inside will irritate and cause discomfort and this is called figging.

Out of sessions and out in the world there is no reason why a slave should be free from Mistress's ministrations. he can be expected to wear a butt plug under his clothes, there for hours or longer at a time. he can have a plug which has electrical contacts on it inserted and can be stimulated with one of the many electro stimulation devices. These can be directly connected with wires to the controller, held by the Mistress or controlled from a remote control device. Electro-stimulation of the anus is possible from the mild like a quiet buzzing effect to the most severe where the slave is shocked so severely that he will fall to the ground with the pain.

It can be fun for Mistress to control a slave with the electrics with the controller in Her hand and the wires under the table out in a restaurant, or to use a remote controller to shock him as he is walking in public. There are even systems which allow remote control by computer from anywhere on the planet and allows a Mistress to keep Her slave under control wherever she may be. There are just so many things that a Mistress can do with Her slave and with his anus.

One recent way in which my Mistress has taken even greater control is with the use of a butt plug worn overnight in bed. When i wake in the night it is there, and i feel filled up inside. It cannot come out. If She uses the electrical butt plug She has a long lead which can go from me to anywhere else in the house and so i can find myself woken with harsh shocks at any time.

The most major effect on me as slave of all of these invasions and toys is that it gives me the opportunity to show my submission to Mistress and to submit to whatever She wants to do. More recently i have discovered that i like it as well, especially the wearing of a butt plug for long periods when at work. Whatever is done it all builds on the total control that Mistress has over my body. It is "Her body" to use and abuse as She wants, and "Her buttocks and anus" to use for Her fun and games. But i do enjoy it all so much as well.

(see also bondage, butt plug, dildo, electrics, figging, remote control, strap on)

B is for bastinado

In Turkish prisons a favourite punishment was to use the bastinado. The subject was secured with his feet in the air and beaten on the soles of the feet with rods or even iron bars. This was very painful and the process caused bruising, damage to the feet and even broken bones so that he was left unable to walk or even crippled for life.

Mistress is never so hard when She hits the feet of a slave. She will use a paddle, a slipper or a cane and it is very painful but there is no long term damage. Still a slave may only be able to hobble around like an old man afterwards for a while.

If Mistress has been wearing high heels or boots and has tender swollen feet She may want to use a slave as a footstool to lift up her legs or require a foot massage. But She might want the slave to feel a little of Her discomfort so She could make him wear shoes or boots that are too tight to make his feet sore or subject him to the bastinado treatment.

(See also: Boots, cane, paddle, punishment, spanking, tawse, whip)

B is for blindfold

When you blindfold a slave you take away their sight and they are placed in the dark. They can no longer see but all other senses become augmented. You can hear more, and become more sensitive to touch whether soft and sensuous or hard and painful. Blindfolds are used a lot with light bondage as part of foreplay by many couples. The blindfold can be made of a tie or scarf, or a travel eye cover collected after a long haul flight. More purpose made blindfolds can be of fabric, leather, or rubber and these are designed so there is no light reaching the eyes of the slave, and no possibility of the blindfold coming off. It is even possible to get totally black contact lenses to remove all sight. Once a slave is put into the dark he is helpless and depends so much more on his Mistress. he can be lead around on a lead, or pulled or pushed to how she wants him. She decides when he is allowed to see again. The longer he is kept in the dark the more it affects him so he no longer has any idea of time or how long he has been kept like that. Long periods of keeping a slave in the dark, overnight or longer will disorientate him and make him unable to tell night from day.

For me there is frustration and pleasure when i am blindfolded. The frustration is that i am not allowed to see Mistress in all Her perfection, and the pleasure is that i know that any touch from Her will have the effect of a powerful shock to my system. i find that being blindfolded and put down and left in bondage at the beginning of a session allows me to relax into the state of bondage, and forget the worries of the day. Long sessions in the dark can be exciting because i do not know what is coming next. i find myself worrying whether i will ever be allowed to see Mistress's face again and begin to lose count of time even when i know that i am safe and helpless under Her control. It is so powerful a tool of subjugation for a Mistress to use on Her slave as it emphasises Her power and my submission.

If the blindfold is combined with a tight hood then the totality of the pressure and the darkness all work together, and if other senses are disabled such as with sounds being played to confuse me then it is even more powerful still. It is amazing to wake in the night blindfolded and to realise that you cannot see, and will not see until Mistress decrees it. The blindfold works on me in this situation to remind me forcibly that i am slave and that Mistress holds all the cards and control over me. Even blindfolded without bondage the blindfold has the effect on me of making me relax into my state of slavery, and wait for Mistress and whatever She has planned for me in her own good time.

i enjoy being blindfolded though there are some who find a blindfold very claustrophobic and difficult to wear. Practice with increasing time blindfolded in an environment where the slave knows he is safe and controlled should allow most slaves to learn to cope, and the longer the blindfold can be used the more powerful its effect.

(See also: darkness and disorientation, hood, isolation, sensory deprivation, training)

B is for Bondage

When i started to be actively interested in bondage it was a largely hidden activity. For me the first experience was being tied up as part of games played as a child. If you have your shoe laces tied together it immobilizes you just as well as any complex bondage system, and makes you submit to the dominant, whether the dominant lady whom any slave might wish to serve, or simply the mate you are playing with in the playground.

For many couples bondage, with one tied spread-eagled to the bed, or with hands tied behind the back can be used to intensify the experience of making love, with the bound partner unable to move and so available for stroking, tickling, and hot and cold stimuli. Especially if the one bound is blindfolded this can be a very intense experience, as without sight , and unable to move, all other sensations, of smell, taste, and especially of touch are enhanced and the pleasure gained from being simply stroked in a sensuous manner when in bondage and blindfolded can be really great giving a totally enjoyable experience. Of course as always it needs to be safe, and consensual, and above all the person bound needs to trust the person who is doing the binding.

In the 50's and 60's pictures of women in bondage circulated more underground than in plain sight, including the celebrated pictures of such bondage models as Betty Page. By the late 60's and early 70's when i started to look at pictures things were different, with magazines showing semi naked women including in bondage poses in magazines available from the nearest newsagents. For a young man the sight of such pictures always caused excitement but it was myself i fantasized into the situations, not me doing the binding.

At that time there were few pictures of men in bondage outside the gay world, and for someone who is straight this was not somewhere i wanted to go. What seemed to excite me was the idea of me being in bondage and controlled by a powerful Mistress, and this was fuelled by magazines such as MADAME.

my first experiences with bondage as a slave were mainly being stretched out on a bed, cuffed to he head and foot of the bed and left, though one early experience had me strapped into a harness and attached to a frame, then hauled up suspended in the harness with my wrists in cuffs attached to the top of the frame, and the legs spread wide. i found this extremely exciting, and it nearly made me come involuntarily. More often the simple act of being in bondage acted to make me more and more excited.

Over the years this has changed, so that now with more experience i find the opposite is true. The excitement is there as i am placed in bondage, mixed with apprehension as to how I may cope with the position and technique chosen by my Mistress. Once the bondage is applied, however, and i am helpless there is a different feeling of release and of freedom. It seems very strange but the act of being made helpless in bondage takes away my freedom and my inhibitions and releases me to the deep relaxation of the freedom just to be and exist, with no decisions as to movement which is curtailed by my bondage or for anything else. i am freed to be a slave and nothing more.

With time the whole bondage picture has come out into he open, especially with the development of Punk in the 1970's and 80's, where stars and fans would dress in new ways, with collars, cuffs and chains to emphasise their difference from the mundane world. Now in 2013 bondage chic, and bondage fashion is everywhere, worn as a fashion statement, a choice for appearance, but also as a direct lifestyle choice.

Similarly the equipment for bondage has become more available, so that everyone can give it a try. Studies suggest that a bondage scenario is one of the more common fantasies for both men and women, with both tying up and being tied up often both desired. The availability of all the equipment now so easily purchased makes this easy to try, so many more people and couples have given it a try to spice up their love life , and to increase their enjoyment. This seems to have exploded since the recent publication of "Fifty Shades of Grey". Although everyday items can so easily be used the availability in most shopping malls of handcuffs, whether furry or plain, bondage rope, and bondage tape in your local "Ann Summers shop" or equivalent gives lots to try out on your partner.

For some people the idea of a lifestyle of bondage or of dominance has also grown, so that whereas many people like a little bondage or domination as part of their life there are some who wish to take it further and i am one of them. For me being in some form of bondage, as much of the time as possible, gives a whole level of enjoyment to my normal and mundane life. Bondage hidden beneath the clothes known only to myself and my Mistress enlivens the day and certainly can make the most boring business meeting more interesting.

Simple household bondage

Although many scenarios use restraint to the corners of a bed, to secure the person in bondage, and spread them out so they can be touched, caressed and handled there are many other pieces of furniture that can so easily be used. Cuffs or rope may seem the "proper "items to use, but most houses have lots of things that can be used to make movement difficult.

Bondage on a chair allows the slave to be secured sitting, with the legs tied to the legs of the chair, and the arms behind the chair or to the arms.

The chair turned upside down gives a structure to which a slave can be bound.

Bondage on a bed can be simply with arms and legs together rather than spread eagled or wrapped in a sheet.

Bondage across a table can lead to good exposure of the backside for a spanking, and also for sex

Bondage with the slave placed in a cupboard or box, small or large allows seclusion out of the way.

The slave can be used to hold up a table top for their Mistress, so that tea may be served on it, and have to keep still, or be used as a candlestick, holding hot candles to provide illumination for their Mistress.

Where the garden is secluded and not overlooked, bondage outside, to a tree, or garden chair is always possible, though difficult if the weather is inclement
so the slave can become wet and cold, which may reduce the pleasure in the scenario for some slaves.. Of course for a slave it is the pleasure of Mistress that counts most.

In the bathroom a slave could be secured with arms around and behind the toilet, forced to kneel and unable to move.

The possibilities in most houses and flats are almost endless, and of course for some people it may be possible to use some space as a playroom, in a spare room, attic, cellar, or garage, where more ambitious bondage arrangements may be made.

The bondage itself can use equally available items. Tying someone's shoelaces together immobilizes them, equally a couple of shoelaces around the wrists and ankles or even tying the thumbs together behind someone's back is equally effective. Most people have scarves and ties which can be used for bondage as well as for clothing. A ball of string is always useful, but so is tape, where a few turns of "sellotape" can immobilise quickly and efficiently.

Although i like more formal bondage, with rope, cuffs, and chains, or the use of handcuffs and leg irons, all of the methods i have mentioned above have given me great pleasure in the past and are always available in most homes and easy to try.

Sometimes bondage can be done without anything, where the slave is required to take a particular position and to hold it, not allowed to move. Here the immobilization is voluntary but none the less real.

Items to signify bondage

By this i mean items commonly worn but which may be used to signify that there is more to them than simple show. Ankle chains are worn on at least one ankle by many women, and they look good in them. They are a simple adornment without significance of bondage. Change the situation a little, and use slightly heavier chains, on both ankles, and the slave is dressed in "slave ankle chains" which can be worn all the time, and mean to both the slave and his Mistress a sign of his slavery.

Similarly many people, both men and women, wear chains around their necks with pendants and charms. Take a heavier chain, locked on and with the key kept by another and it becomes a mark of slavery. Dog collars and other studded collars are often part of a "punk "like appearance, but there is no reason why the collar cannot be locked on, and come with a lead to use in private. Of course it is not always possible to show such things at work or outside, but for a man dressed in a suit there is no reason why underneath he cannot be wearing ankle chains and collar to signify to himself and his Mistress his slave state.

i was introduced to collars and chains first during sessions of bondage, but later my Mistress started to send me out to run errands for her in bondage under my clothes, and then introduced me to the wearing of a cock and ball ring, made of stainless steel, to be worn under my clothes and labelled with my Mistress's name and my slave name.

Later i was introduced a rubber collar to wear under my shirt, and thin gold ankle chains to wear under my socks each day. These signified to me my state as slave, and kept it always in my mind but did not limit me or prevent movement.

Most recently my Mistress has changed the rubber collar for a steel collar which is invisible under my shirt and tie, locked on, a chain with an identity disk for the neck and heavy silver ankle chains which are heavy enough to be always felt as I walk. The collar feels heavy and slightly reduces my neck movement. The two together feel really good. Sometimes i am in wrist chains as well. These are signs of my slavery hidden to the outside world but real to me and Mistress, and compliment the wearing of a steel chastity device.

I have found that being cuffed with steel cuffs, whether to the wrists or ankles always triggers in me the desire to submit, and the possibility of them being used on me excites just as much as their use. It is their heaviness and the fact that they are completely inescapable that make them for me successful as a bondage tool.

Positions for bondage

There are so many positions that can be used for bondage, especially with rope bondage, that it is impossible to enumerate them all. Many books on bondage show people in all sorts of twisted and stretched positions, but some of them require a yoga-like level of ability to contort the body. The difficulty is that the more strained the position the more difficult it is to hold the position and to cope with it in bondage for any length of time. If it has taken a long time to set the slave into the position and they can only hold it for a few minutes then it may not be successful.

If cramps occur, and the slave cannot move these can be very painful. When i started as a slave i would often not have enough to drink before a session and was prone to develop cramps in my legs. This gave occasionally such severe pain that the session and position had to be abandoned which was a pity.

As in so many things, practice and experimentation improve performance. Finding positions which can be held, for longer periods and practising with them allows them to be used for longer and intensified. Originally i found the standard hogtie position with me on my face, hands behind back and attached to the ankles pulled up to join them very difficult, and i could scarcely stand it for a few minutes. Now with practice, and in an attempt to please my Mistresses i find that i can cope with it for longer, and once in the position have learned to relax into the bondage, allowing it to be tightened to produce a tighter and more pleasing effect

Of course sometimes the Mistress may want to put the slave into a position that is difficult as a form of punishment. This needs to be agreed beforehand, and the bondage needs to be secured in such a way it can be quickly released if there is distress and it is too much. As always allowing someone to tie you up or put you into any bondage is a matter of consent and trust,

Experience

One thing that i have learned about bondage, over the years and from the various Mistresses that have trained me is that different Mistresses enjoy different forms of bondage, and have more experience with one way than another. That is one of the fun things about bondage. Over time you are trained on different methods all with the same end in mind, the total subjugation of the slave to his Mistress. you can be introduced to such a range of differing methods of making it difficult for you to move and find out what you enjoy and what your Mistress enjoys, and explore ever more and more methods and positions.

my Journey

Over the past years i have travelled a significant distance in my experience of bondage and my appreciation and pleasure at being in bondage. i have moved from no bondage, through sessions of increasing complexity to a position where i am in daily bondage with collar, chastity, and ankle chains, and more whenever possible , often for days at a time.

The original sessions tended to be short, no more than an hour, but now i crave long periods in bondage, and multiple positions and techniques, with an average session of over four hours plus time in bondage travelling to and from the location, and occasional sessions of 24 hours or longer whenever this becomes possible. There is more and more time involved, more and more learning how to be in a bondage state, and above all more and more pleasure in the submission that bondage brings.

The issues are to make the bondage relatively comfortable, unless it is being used for punishment, totally inescapable and secure. Once in such bondage i can relax into a state of bliss and timelessness, especially if isolated and blindfolded, existing in the moment and waiting for whatever comes next. The better the equipment used the more pleasurable it can be, but it is not the equipment that gives this. It is the care and the imagination used by my Mistress and the development of my relationship as a slave that leads to the best sessions and times in bondage.

(See also: blindfolds, body bag, bondage at work, cages, chains, confinement in a car trunk, collars, cupboards, cuffs, gags, handcuffs, hoods, humbler, isolation, leash, leg irons, manacles, mummification, overnight sessions, predicament bondage, pervertable, posture collar, pressure, rack, restraint, rope, stocks, stress position, suspension, training, torment and torture, weights, X position for bondage)

B is for Body bag

A body bag is a bag in which the body of a slave may be pack away securely. The body bags used by the police for dead bodies cover the whole body including the head but those used on slaves usually stop at the neck to allow the slave to breathe. Some bags are no more than a simple bag, with a zip out of reach of the slave so once in it he cannot escape, but others have a variety of zips so that the Mistress can access the groin, nipples, or backside with the slave still secure inside.

The best bags have internal sleeves so that the slave has arms secured so that he cannot touch himself and has no possibility of being able to reach any of the zips.
Bags need to be robustly constructed so that even if a slave struggles the bag will not tear or break.

Bags are particularly good for long periods of bondage, where the slave is expected to remain restrained for hours at a time, and are often used for overnight bondage. A slave fully secured in the bag cannot escape, yet is able to lie flat and so can be left on the floor overnight or for even longer periods. If he is hooded or blindfolded as well then bondage is total. It is for this reason that they are sometimes described as "sleep sacks "in catalogues of bondage gear.

Bags are available in a variety of materials. A canvas bag will be robust but itchy and of only moderate price whilst one made of heavy leather will be smooth inside, totally fitting to the body, and very expensive. Rubber can be used but there are risks that the slave may get too hot or too cold depending on the environment, and a slave left for hours is a rubber bag may begin to sweat a lot, and almost become "boiled in the bag"
There are latex bags which are inflatable so the slave is held inside a pressurized bag, and alternatively it is possible to vacuum pack a

slave with a vacuum bag instead. One relatively new form of bag is that made of an elastic material, either elastane or darlex which is stronger. The slave can try to move and struggle, but the elasticity of the bag springs back so his struggles are in vain.

my experience of being bagged goes back many years, and it is always a pleasure to be placed in a bag and hooded. When this happens i know that i am in for a prolonged period in bondage and am likely to be left on my own. i am usually hooded or blindfolded as well, so it feels very secure and i have no idea of time passing. By the time Mistress releases me, or opens one of the zips to access my parts for torment, i am often slightly disorientated with no idea of whether I have been in the bag for minutes or hours, and this is certainly the case if i am put in the bag overnight. It is such a good system for sensory deprivation and a safe way to confine a slave.

If the Mistress wishes the bag can be made tighter with the addition of straps or rope and this can also be used to secure the bag in place. It is possible to transport a slave in a bondage bag in the boot of a car, and he is certainly not going to escape. For slaves at home with their Mistress a bondage bag is a good place for the slave to be placed routinely for sleep overnight, as unless the bag is too tight, or very hot or cold sleep is possible. The slave can be bagged and left on the floor next to Mistress's bed, or placed somewhere else in another room or a cupboard.

Once in the bag there is no escape, and Mistress can use the bag as a footstool, or poke at it with her feet or heels. If the slave is connected to an electrical stimulation device they can be shocked, and if there are zips or flaps over vulnerable areas they can be accessed. Putting a slave in a bondage bag makes them totally secure and vulnerable for all a Mistress may wish to do with them.

That is why a bondage bag is such a useful addition to add to the equipment a Mistress may use even though it is expensive. If well looked after it can be used for years, and the rubber bag mistress uses on me is over 10 years old, but still working well both as a bag, and also when inflated as well.

(See also: bondage, compressive clothing, confinement in a car boot, disorientation, isolation, latex, leather, mummification, rubber, pressure, sensory deprivation)

B is for Bondage at work

Bondage is something that most slaves experience in sessions with their Mistress and also away from work during evenings, nights and weekends. But i am controlled with bondage all the rest of the time as well. Only this is bondage hidden under my clothing and invisible to the outside world.

When i get up in the morning i put on my steel chastity, and my silver ankle chains, and collar. i wear a silver chain around my neck from which hangs a dogtag which proclaims my slave name and the Logo of my Mistress. Luckily i always wear a collar and tie at work, so this is all hidden.

From time to time Mistress orders me to wear my butt plug all day, and this is often when i have important meetings to address. Most recently i was lecturing to several hundred Engineering students at my old University, and once Mistress heard of this She required me to do so in the butt plug to be worn all day. Certainly standing there in the plug and chastity felt so different, and exciting, from when i sat there as a student and reminded me all the time that i am her slave and property.

Over time Mistress has added to my bondage. i had rashly described how tight i found the stockings i had worn on a transatlantic flight to try to reduce the risk of a clot in my legs. Now i have to wear women's tights, and not just tights, but ones with
"support" which means elastane to make them even tighter. i put them on first thing in the morning and wear them all day. When i try to walk fast it is difficult and my gait has become much shorter with smaller steps as otherwise the elastic pulls my thighs together. If i sit down i feel them crushing my thighs and calves, and if i walk, particularly up stairs, it makes things so much more difficult.

The high waist rolls down to form a stiff band around my stomach, which feels as if there is a tight chain there all the time.

This was all new and means even more bondage control over me at work all day every day, But none of it is visible, so i wear it and it makes me think of Mistress all the time, as it is designed to do. Next Mistress wanted me to change from size large to size medium, and this was be even tighter. She also mentioned the use of control
pants " Spanx" used by ladies to make them look smaller, and which She thinks will work well to control a slave and keep him from eating too much. Once these arrived i was put to wear a tight elastane vest and boxer shorts in addition to all my other bondage to wear at work. Even more recently a corset has been added too.

Now i live my life at work in bondage. The only times i am allowed to be freed from it are at home and if i have to take a flight somewhere and cannot wear the steel chastity and butt plug or collar through security. Apart from that it is every day, all day. i carry the items with me in hand luggage and put them on after i have gone
through security, but i am sometimes allowed to carry a key with me to take them off if necessary. Normally any keys are left at home and there is no possibility of release from the bondage.

i do enjoy bondage so much, and have had such good times tied up over the years but now bondage has intruded into every area of my life, and it is so, so, good. It feels right to be wearing my slave identity around my neck with a collar tight around my neck. It is right that i be kept in chastity in the steel device whose key is left at home, so i cannot flirt with anyone at work, and am reminded whenever i think sexual thoughts that my parts are fully controlled.

The ankle chains emphasise my position as a slave, and the tights are a new way to subjugate me, and have me even more held in control.

i wonder what new bondage She will think of next for me to wear at work. Her imagination is boundless, and Her ideas lead to me being ever more and more in thrall to Her and more fully her slave and property

(See also: bondage, butt plug, chains, collar, corset, training, work)

B is for Boots

All women look naturally more imposing when they wear boots, and particularly if they are boots with a high and spiky heel. Many slaves, of whom i am one, have found that pictures of a Mistress in boots are exciting, but that the presence of a booted Mistress is more exciting still.

For some this is a fetish, where they can only be excited at the appearance of a woman wearing boots, but for most of us the appearance is exciting but it is only part of the excitement. Some slaves wish to spend all their time at the feet of a Mistress kissing and licking Her boots. Others like to be made to clean muck off the boots of their Mistress with their tongue.

But it all depends on what Mistress wants. i love to see Mistress dressed to express Her dominance, including boots, but it is more important to me that i am allowed to see Mistress at all. For me She looks magnificent whatever She may be wearing.

i enjoy being permitted to kneel before Mistress and to kiss Her boots, Her shoes, or even Her feet and to do anything for Her. If She wants Her feet massaged then it is a total pleasure to me. Does it matter what She is wearing? No it is Who is doing the wearing that counts above everything, but it is still nice to be there kissing the toes and the heels of her boots. She has allowed me to do this and i am so grateful.

Some slaves are required to clean the boots and shoes of their Mistress as part of their daily work, and expected to polish the shoes with their tongue. Others are made to lick the shoes to polish off boot polish already applied. If Mistress has been out walking and it has been muddy or dirty outside then it is a reasonable request that her slave should clean her boots, though whether She wants this done with his mouth or with brushes and cloths is irrelevant. i look forward to the day when Mistress may require me to clean her dirty boots with my mouth as i kneel before her. But it is what She wants that matters not what a slave wants. A slave should be there to serve Mistress in any way She wishes, not to be given pleasure for his particular kinks.

Making a slave kneel in public to clean the bottom of a Mistress's boots can also be seen as a humiliating exercise for the slave, but this may be important to show him his proper place at the feet of Mistress.

(See also: domestic service, foot worship, humiliation, personal service).

B is for Branding

A slave may be marked in a number of ways to show he is the slave and property of his Mistress. Branding is one of these methods but it is rarely practiced in the United Kingdom for here it is considered by the law as a form of actual bodily harm and a criminal offence to do it or to have it done on you. Other countries have different rules.

In slavery as practiced in the past which was totally non–consensual it was common for slaves and property to be branded. Some slaves were branded even on the face which was completely barbaric. This was horrible. In fully consensual BDSM things are different for here it is the slave who often begs to be branded and marked as the property of his Mistress, and it is in this context that marks and brands are applied.

The process tends to use a wire or brand, heated to scorch and burn the skin and produce a mark which will then cause a scar to develop. The risks of infection of the skin which has been burned and damaged is very real, even if the maximum attempts are made to keep everything clean and dry. It can also be very painful and there is an additional risk of bleeding. Some scars will fade but others are there for life, and may be difficult to explain to a partner in the future, or risky to show in public

So there are good reasons why few slaves are branded. Alternatively the slave and Mistress may decide to use a tattoo, which will leave a permanent mark, and this is something which can be used to show the Mistress's name, or logo, or heraldic device or any other pattern which seems right to use.

i have not been branded but i do have a small scar where play with candles has caused a mark. i am known to have it by my family but they do not know its significance or how it was produced. For me it is a brand to show i belong to Mistress as her slave and She knows it too.

(See also: contracts, ownership, tattoos)

B is for Brazilian wax

Slaves need to have their body prepared as Mistress wants and this may include having all hair removed from the cock and balls and any other part of the body. Some Mistresses like to have a slave completely without hair and have all body hair removed regularly to give a smooth surface. There are some whose slaves are expected to shave their heads as well. This shows Her power over the slaves in a very concrete way.

For a slave wearing a chastity device, hair around the genital area tends to get in the way, and makes keeping clean more difficult so genital shaving is often required by the slave and inspected by his Mistress.

Taking things one stage further some Mistresses require that the slave attends regularly for a Brazilian wax treatment. This involves the use of hot wax, applied to the skin then allowed to harden and pulled off pulling out the hairs as it does so. This is applied to the cock, the balls, and the crack around the anus and through to the back and prepares the slave so that Mistress can enjoy herself playing with these areas. It is possible to have the pubic hairs removed with the same technique and this is termed a "Hollywood" waxing treatment. This treatment takes up to an hour and can be quite painful as the hairs are pulled out.

Waxing to remove genital hair is common for women and there are a large number of beauty therapists who provide this service. Many women want their pubic hair and genital hair trimmed and treated as they want it, and Mistresses may want to take the same approach with a slave. Fewer therapists provide a service for men, but it is always possible to find someone through the internet or Yellow Pages.

It is quite a step for a man to have his hair removed on the orders of his Mistress. The process is not comfortable, and it is very exposed to lie there with all your parts hanging out and the hair being pulled out area by area. Many slaves find the loss of their hair humiliating and the feeling that part of your manhood has been removed.

Others enjoy being waxed to show their Mistress that they are obedient to Her wishes.

Of course once shaving or waxing has started it need to continue regularly otherwise the hairs grow back, so it becomes a regular duty and is expected by Mistress to show a slave submits to Her. So the slave becomes hairless there for ever.

In some ways having your hairs waxed away is no different than accepting the style of haircut Your Mistress desires You have, or having Your eyebrows trimmed as she orders. Many men who are not slaves submit to a partner who decides when they go for a haircut and how much hair comes off, and a few accompany their men to make sure this happens. Waxing is just more of the same and signifies that a slave is prepared to have his body changed to suit his Mistress.

So waxing to please Your Mistress can become a regular part of a slave's life.

My experience with waxing has come late in my time as a slave. It was only a year ago that Mistress started to require me to shave my balls for Her and there was always the situation that the shaving was not as complete as She desired. As a result She decided that i should have my hairs removed with a Brazilian wax technique. The plan was for Her to accompany me to hold my hand and make sure it was done to Her satisfaction. But She gave me a letter to the therapist giving her orders for me in case She could not attend. On the day She was stuck in traffic so i had to go in on my own and hand over the letter.

i arrived at the therapist She had booked for me and handed over the letter. It was all very professional and an hour later i left waxed and with all the hair removed on my cock, balls and the crack through to the back, and also from my nipples. The letter had made clear that i was the slave of Mistress and that she required this of me, and i was happy that the therapist was happy with this. i left to attend Mistress and be inspected by Her to make sure the work was done to her satisfaction. i also had to demonstrate that the next treatment was already booked.

Now this has become a regular part of my preparation for Mistress. i may not be branded as Her slave, but my hair is removed to demonstrate that She has total control over my cock , balls, backside and nipples. It still feels strange to lie there and have the hairs pulled out, but i know i am preparing to serve Mistress as She wants and that is what counts.

(See also: contracts, domination, forced feminization, humiliation, ownership, sissy, submission, wax)

B is for breath control

Breathing is essential for life so anything that makes breathing more difficult for a slave may be dangerous. Placing a slave in a plastic bag so they cannot breathe properly leads to an inability for them to get oxygen in or carbon dioxide out, and can lead to death so this is not a good idea.

But Mistresses can have control over many aspects of a slave's breathing without there being significant danger. There must always be a way for the slave to breathe without difficulty, no matter how he is gagged or hooded, and no slave who is gagged should be left alone in case he is sick and inhales his vomit closing off the airway.

But if the slave is hooded, or made to breathe through a tube Mistress can control his breathing if he is happy with this. She can suddenly cover his mouth or the breathing tube so he cannot get air in or out and just as suddenly remove the block to breathing. For a few seconds the slave will not be able to breathe which will not harm him, but he will have learned that Mistress is in control.

If She wants she can put Her own mouth up against the end of the breathing hole or tube, and breathe in Herself through Her nose, and breathe out through Her mouth into the slave. He will have to coordinate his breathing to Hers and each time She breathes out he will breathe in air warmed directly from Her. He will know that the air comes from his Mistress, and breathe in the aromas of Her who controls him. This is safe, possible, and so very intimate, but it is the Mistress who is in control, and is controlling every breath that the slave takes.

For slaves breathing control is also important when they are being stimulated by their Mistress. If the slave starts to pant he will find the pain of a flogging may seem less. If he times his breathing in to the time of a stroke of the cane it is sometimes easier to bear. But if he pants too much this will blow off too much carbon dioxide and lead to dizziness or even feeling woozy as the slave is hyperventilating.

For me having my breathing controlled by Mistress when i am hooded and She puts Her mouth to the breathing hole and breathes out so i can breathe in her air, warmed and caressed by her lungs is a very intimate act. i love it but would only be happy doing this with someone i trust absolutely, and we have years of me being Her slave which have built this trust.

Outside of breathing controlled by the Mistress who holds power over the slave learning to breathe slowly and in synchrony with your partner when the one is curled up in contact with the other is a way to share even the frequency and pattern of breathing between two people. you fit your breathing pattern consciously to that of Your partner, and breathe together as one; so intimate.

(See also: gags and gagging, hoods)

B is for Butt plugs

A butt plug is a plug which can be worn by a slave pushed up inside his butt. They come in varying sizes and shapes, and some are shaped so as to stimulate the prostrate gland on the front wall of the back passage, whilst others are more spherical in shape.

A Mistress may wish a slave to be trained to wear a butt plug to make it easier for Her to insert things of ever increasing size into his anus. She may also want the slave to wear a plug so he is always aware that Mistress controls this part of him as well as all the rest. He can start by being required to wear a pad of toilet paper inside his pants to remind him of this then expected to insert a plug each day and keep it in. This is different from what is done with dildos and many other items inserted rectally which are only in for short periods.

Although many butt plugs are sold for long term use they can rarely be worn for more than 12 hours, otherwise the backup of waste products above the plug can lead to an accident and leakage. So the plug needs to come out to go to the toilet at least twice a day. If the slave has been prepared for the plug by being given a large volume enema to empty out his bowel and is put onto a liquid diet then the plug can stay in longer.

It is a sign of slavery to be required to wear a plug, and being trained to take ever larger ones prepares the slave for greater obedience to his Mistress. Some plugs have electrodes on their surface so can be used to give a slave shocks inside. When the power of the shocks reaches a maximum the whole buttock area as well as the anus all contract in time to the shocks. Mistress can control the size and frequency of the shocks via a wire and controller or sometimes with a remote controller.

Mistress started me on wearing a butt plug some years ago, initially for sessions, then for use more frequently out of sessions, and particularly when giving talks in public. She likes the idea of me standing there in front of hundreds giving a lecture with a plug inside me. Now i am expected to wear a plug as much as possible, and the size is increasing. i wear one all night in bed.

This is yet another way in which i am able to show my submission to Mistress and my obedience to Her wishes and orders. She knows it reminds me that all of me is Hers to play with as She wishes, and so i obey and wear my plug, even though it is uncomfortable especially on sitting down. Driving long distances in a plug is something i have gradually got used to; it is never comfortable, but then why should i expect it to be comfortable.

(See also: arse, electrics, dildo, training, power, submission)

C is for Chastity

There are books and articles written about male chastity though much of what is found on the internet is fiction and not fact. If you are considering the use of male chastity in the life for any male it is a good idea to seek information from a number of separate sources.

"Restart Intimacy(Amazon and Kindle) by Ms Sierra Parker gives a good introduction to the whole subject, and Her book "Re-introduction to Intimacy; Build the Foundations" shows how to develop male chastity in a relationship, with exercises to do, and a process to follow which will led to full chastity for the man. Lucy Fairbourne in her book "Male Chastity; a guide for Key-holders" looks at male chastity from the standpoint of the woman, and Sarah Jameson on her website malechastityblog.com has books and articles to help a man in a relationship move to male chastity. But this is not quite the same in a Mistress/slave relationship where the power exchange between the slave giving up power and the Mistress taking up the power over the slave makes for a slightly different dynamic.

So what is male chastity?   Male chastity is the situation in which a man hands over the control and access to his penis and testicles to another. He may refrain from ejaculation voluntarily, and stop any masturbation, and agree to do this for his partner or Mistress. He gives the decision of when he is allowed to ejaculate or have an orgasm freely, and she decides when this may occur.

This approach, where an agreement is made that the man will enter chastity for a period, and except when his partner or Mistress wants it he will refrain from ejaculation can work, but for many men this "honour "system is not enough, for there is always the option for them to cheat and to masturbate on their own without their partner knowing.

For this reason an alternative method to ensure chastity is for the man to wear a device which surrounds his penis and prevents it becoming enlarged or him ejaculating. This is a lockable male chastity device, and typically consists of a ring which fits around the base of the penis underneath the balls, and a cage or tube which is locked onto this. The device is locked into place and the man can then no longer masturbate, ejaculate, touch his penis or take it off. The key for the lock is handed over to his Mistress who then controls his penis and his ejaculation. This is a voluntary act in which the man shows his trust and hands over the key to his most precious possessions to Her who will then decide when he is to be released. This is an action which gives enormous power to the woman who controls him so it is often a part of life for a male slave.

There is consent, and if he consents that he can be kept in it even when he begs to be released then this is consensual as well. He will need encouragement to persevere in its use from his Mistress and there are so many ways She can encourage him.

There are problems here, as most devices are difficult to use to pass urine standing up and he may have to sit to pass urine or he will make a mess. Having a device locked around your private parts the device may rub and become sore, so it is often necessary to experiment to find one that fits and is comfortable. Cleaning the area may not be so easy, but it is always possible, and your Mistress does not want you smelling or getting unwell or having a sore.

Work is rarely an issue, as the devices fit easily under clothing and are invisible. No one knows how many men on the train are locked into chastity, or if anyone at work is in a similar position. This gives a feeling of being "special" and having a secret life, and this can be arousing as well. Travel is more of a problem, especially with belt type devices and those that are steel or have metal locks as you cannot wear them and go through airport security without setting off the alarms.

No matter as you can take them off and put on after you have passed through security and you are certainly not going to be masturbating or need your penis functional when you are going through the security system. With the use of the plastic CB range and a numbered plastic lock this is rarely an issue as there is no metal lock to set off detectors.

Sport can be an issue, particularly with contact sports, where you do not want your colleagues to suddenly realise you have steel balls. For cycling and horse riding not all devices are comfortable.

Sometimes, even with the best will in the world, and total determination to succeed he will not be able to wear a device, because it always makes him so sore. This can be a reason not to stop the process but to find something else that works and does not cause these problems but can be worn at work without difficulty. Even here a combination of times wearing the device and times out of it but held on his "honour" to male chastity may get round the problem, and if there is a will to succeed then things do work out well. Failure occurs when the will and the drive to succeed are not there, and this is down to the individual and how much effort he wants to put into the relationship with his Mistress.

In the first stage of moving into a life of male chastity the slave needs to have a full discussion with his Mistress so he understands what he is getting into, and may need to experiment with periods of virtual chastity when he does not masturbate for a whole week, then discusses the difficulties with Mistress.

In the next stage the slave will be expected to obtain a device to use to control him and to get used to wearing it, though there are some Mistresses who will provide a device for a fee. Now is the time to purchase equipment and to start using it.

It is important to note that any device should be safe, and not pinch or cause irritation to the skin; it must be comfortable so the man can work in it and live his daily life. It must be convenient and fit under his clothes so it is not apparent when he is outside, and it should also look OK. One element which is vital is that it should be secure, so he cannot take it off, so the lock does hold it in place, and so that it performs its assigned task of keeping him locked away as is required.

Once the man and his Mistress have chosen and purchased the equipment there will be time to learn how to fit it, and how to wear it for longer and longer periods. Although most sources on male chastity devices claim that they can be worn, locked on and left, it is rare for this to be the case, and time needs to be spent making sure that the parts all fit together, it can be worn, and that it works and cannot come off. Many who have worn male chastity devices for many years as part of a male chastity lifestyle still report that it took a few weeks before they had the right device for them and it fitted well and they could relax into its wear. These are people who have succeeded with male chastity but still it took them time.

Introduction of anything new takes time to implement so there is a need for regular review of what has happened. This should happen every week to start with and then less often as needed, but if problems, particularly practical problems, arise, then a discussion may be urgent, particularly if the man cannot cope because of some problem of his general health or particular soreness of the device which might need adjustment.

One way to secure the device is with a numbered plastic lock, so that if the device ahs to come off for any reason then the slave can inform the mistress, and change to another lock as soon as the problem is sorted out. This might be a visit to the doctor for a medical examination or something similar. This way the mistress will know he ha been out of the device. The slave can be expected to provide photographic evidence that he is locked into the chastity device to his Mistress at any time when She will be able to check the lock has not been changed.

Once the device is fully in use the slave and Mistress may now proceed to a chastity contract which will allow the slave to be kept in chastity for a defined period and formalise the arrangement.

My experience with being is chastity started many years ago. i was introduced to the CB www.cb-x.com range of plastic devices and expected to wear one for sessions and then for longer periods between sessions. Mistress and i experimented with a number of devices, including one with electrodes attached to it which allow Mistress to shock me from a distance, and can even be controlled via computer and internet connection. This was theDL2000 from www.Dreamloverlabs.com.

Now for the past few years i have worn a steel device with a ring which fits around the base of the penis and is secured to a tube which covers the shaft of the penis and is closed off with a small 6mm hole to allow me to pass urine. The device is secure and i cannot get it off, and heavy so i always know it is there. Mistress requires me to wear it all day every day, but it comes off at night for a wash, and if i am away from home then the device is on 24/7 with Mistress holding the only key. The result is that Mistress controls my chastity all the time, and that masturbation is forbidden totally, and has been for the past 20 months.

It is not easy as things do get sore, and if i become aroused when in the device it feels as if my penis is being crushed as is the case. When i have been allowed to ejaculate the system still works, but only when Mistress decides. i have fully consented to this and continue to do so. it has become a major part of my life as a slave. One major effect of wearing the chastity device and being under these rules is that i become ever more attentive to Mistress. i know that in all things i must submit and obey her and i must not get Her unhappy with me and my performance. If i fail then there is the risk that i may be subject to Her judgement and the device may stay on for longer. i want to do my best, but i know that i will be held to that and it changes the way i behave and improves me. This is just one of the many ways in which Mistress is changing me and improving me and my behaviour.

(See also: chastity contract, chastity devices, ownership, power exchange, submission, training)

C is for Chastity Contract

A slave who has been introduced to male chastity by his Mistress will move to being under a chastity contract to define his situation. This is a similar contract to that which he may have for his slavery as a whole, but because male chastity is such a specific part of his being a slave there is often a specific contract to cover this as well.

A contract allows the slave and the Mistress to discuss its contents and the consequences of signing a contract with the responsibilities both will have for each other. It sets things out formally, and allows a formal though non-legally binding agreement between them and makes sure that the consent of the slave to his slavery and in this case his chastity is fully understood, explicit and agreed.

Initially this contract will only be for a limited period of a few weeks but then when it is seen by both the Mistress and the slave to work it can be renewed for a longer period. Most chastity contracts need to be reconsidered at yearly intervals. The only situation when a contract is no longer of use is when the slave moves from being a slave to a deeper level of slavery where he becomes the property of his Mistress. Then there cannot be a contract which supposes that both parties are free to sign, but a memorandum of understanding so that both Mistress and slave know the situation.

Here is a sample contract, with the name Michael used for the slave who is agreeing to be placed in chastity for a period.

Sample Male Chastity Contract

This is a contact of male chastity between Michael and his Mistress.

Michael agrees to enter male chastity, whether with his penis and ball sack locked in a male chastity device or whether he is without any device but held on his honour not to masturbate or ejaculate.

The Mistress agrees to be his key holder and to supervise his male chastity and to support him through the process and when there are difficulties.

Michael agrees that he will be kept in total chastity with no opportunity to ejaculate or orgasm except when the Mistress gives explicit permission for him to be released.

The Mistress agrees that she will be open and fair to Michael in deciding on any release, but may tease him, suggest possible release then decide against it, and make her own decisions on when she wants him released.

Michael agrees that even if he begs for release or to be unlocked this will only occur if his Mistress decides it, unless there are extenuating circumstances including illness, accident, disease, or injury.
He realises that begging for release may lead to his period in the device being prolonged. He also realises that he may be sentenced to further periods in chastity if he displeases or fails his Mistress in any way
Michael will be permitted to be unlocked to attend medical examinations or to pass through airport type

security but the device must be re applied once this has happened.

The Mistress promises to support Michael in all his endeavours in male chastity to the fullest extent possible,

Michael can beg for an extension of the period in male chastity at any time but this will not be enacted without a specific discussion and agreement of the conditions of this extension

The Mistress has unconditional and irrevocable control of Michael's orgasms and can permit or deny them for any reason at any time.

Conditions of release are at the Mistress's sole discretion but it is not intended that this contract will lead to cessation of orgasms for Michael, only that they will be under the total control of the Mistress.

This contract will last from   .. /.. /....

Until   .. / .. /....

And is agreed by both of the parties

Signed   Supervisor/Mistress
Dated

Signed   Michael
Dated

This is a sample contract, and details will be different for different people. Some will want as much as possible made explicit, and others will want to leave more unwritten.

If you look through all the clauses you will see the magnitude of the step that Michael and his Mistress are taking, and they are only doing so after carrying out periods of chastity as a trial. They have already identified that this is something he wants to do, and he realises the size of the commitment they are making. That is why they are writing it out in the form of a legal contract.

Of course such contracts are dependant upon consent of both parties, and the continuation of such consent. They have no basis in law but are an important exhibition of the dynamic which links the Mistress and slave together.

C is for Chastity devices

There are a wide range of chastity devices available on the market. The one simple rule is that the cheaper they are the more likely to break or to fail. There are very cheap made devices costing £10-20 ($15-300 but these are often no good. Most slaves find that the plastic devices of the CB range are good to use to start, though some find these too easy to remove. There are also more secure systems made of surgical grade steel, or those which incorporate a belt type design. You can even buy one on Amazon.

Here are a number of sources of information that you may find useful.

www.lovehoney.co.uk
www.cb-x.com
www.tollyboy.com
www.chastityheaven.com
www.wikepedia.org/chastitybelt
www.malechastitylifestyle.com
www.steelpleasures.com
i started with one of the CB designs, but now have been moved to a steel tube from
which is relatively comfortable, and easy to wear for long periods. Cleaning is a difficulty sometimes so it probably needs removal approximately once every week or two under supervision.

No man can be forced into a chastity device. Even the most secure has a lock which can be sawn off if the slave really wishes to come out of it, but obviously tampering with the device, taking it off , or removing the lock when not allowed to do so by Mistress is a serious crime and can lead to the slave being dismissed. That is why a male slave should take time to get into male chastity, and consider what he is doing, try devices, and settle on one that works and can be worn for long periods before long periods of locking up start. In fiction the lock goes on and it is for good; in reality it is a process and a learning curve for everyone, even the Mistress

C is for cage

i enjoy being kept in bondage, and few things speak more of bondage than a cage in which a slave can be incarcerated. The slave is pushed into the cage, often already in chains and hooded, and kneels there to hear the ominous sound as the cage door shuts and the click as the lock is locked and the key removed. he knows that this is where he will be staying for some time, hours and hours, or even longer, and that there is no escape.

i have always felt like this when being shut in a cage from the first time i experienced one. Mistress used to have a chamber with a standing cage and a classic puppy cage with a bondage table on top. i could be placed in the standing cage facing the wall with my hands secured behind me, and know that i would have to remain standing like that until released. Not able to turn round, not able to move, must remain standing, pressed against the hard cold wall. A few hours of that and i would do anything to be released and move around.

Alternatively i would be pushed into the other cage, kneeling and hooded, and be left. This had hard steel bars but it was possible to get on my side and curl in a ball, or lie on my back with my feet up or kneeling with my head bowed to the floor.

The possibility of movement meant that i was able to cope when Mistress used it overnight or for a whole day, as i was able to move a little, and could even put my feet between the bars to straighten my legs, unless the ankles were secured to prevent this. This was so secure i could be left in it in an outbuilding whilst Mistress went off to Her bed to sleep.

Not all that easy, especially if it was very cold, but i was often allowed a rug to cover myself to stop getting too cold, but also often hooded or blindfolded to have no idea of the passage of time, only the sound of the birds outside and the traffic to tell me that it was morning eventually.

Being in the cage also allowed Mistress other options, whether She wanted to shock me with electrics on my cock, balls, or through a butt plug, or applying heating cream to all the sensitive areas before incarceration.

On one memorable day the cage was filled with nettles and i was required to turn over and over until all parts had been stung, and then left to the pain of the stings kneeling there in a hood. Cages have also played their part when we have used outside dungeons to play. At one place there was a small bird cage in which i had to sit with my knees up to my head, and be left, and also an outside cage in which i was placed one frosty morning naked and in chains.

More recently Mistress moved to a house without space for a formal dungeon chamber, but which did have a cupboard under the stairs. i produced a cage gate and frame which was then built into the space, leaving a triangular space under the stairs which could be locked, and also walled off with a thick board to make things even more secure. The cupboard door could then be locked and i was on my own in chains.

This was used for periods of several hours, but overnight the cage door was left unlocked and hinged up, and i was allowed to sleep in, allowing me to stretch out to full length, just, but still with the cupboard door locked and me inside.

Being left caged, chained up, and in the total darkness of a hood, in a darkened cage, is very powerful. i find i rapidly have no idea of how long i have been there, and it could be hours or minutes. No matter for i am going to stay there until Mistress decides. It forces me to accept my position of slavery and bondage. It releases me from the other worries of the day. A period in the cupboard or cage cleanses my mind and puts me almost into a trance.

One other cage owned by Mistress is a collapsible dog cage, bought from a pet shop. This can be erected in a couple of minutes and me put inside. This cage is much more difficult for it is so small i can only kneel and crouch down with my head bowed. The wrists, ankles, and collar can also be attached to the cage with quickly applied plastic ties, so i am held in the position my Mistress desires. Just to make things even more difficult garden canes can be threaded through the cage to restrict my movement still further. Here movement is so restricted that i can only stay in this cage for a much shorter time, and after an hour cramps begin to be a problem.

When Mistress says She wants me put down for a period or for the night i am always both excited and scared. i will have no idea of time, i will have limited movement, and i will stay where i am put. It excites me that She has taken such a level of control over me, and is showing Her power. The sound of the key in the lock as i am locked away excites me with the fear of what is to come. The knowledge that i will be staying in the cage for a long time excites me as i will be helpless and anything can happen; Mistress might forget to come back for me, even though i know that this is impossible and i am safe.

If You can get hold of a cage, or turn a small and cramped cupboard into a place of bondage you can have so much fun, over hours and days. Time caged excites, calms, and prepares a slave for what is to come whether a period of serving Mistress or a severe flogging.

The caging is dramatic with the door shutting and the click of the lock and removal of the key. The release is a release into a wider world as the slave crawls on all fours out into the blinding light or remains hooded for his next torment. Release itself is disconcerting as after a period in the total darkness of a cage and hood the slave often has no idea what is coming next. This is my experience and it all makes whatever happens next more of a shock, even if i have been told of it in advance.

Slaves require caging and all that comes with it to remind them that they are slave and not free, and the use of a pet cage compares them to animal not human. It is such a good way for a Mistress to show Her power, and gives her opportunity to do other things whilst the slave is in the cage, whether to deal with other slaves or just to relax, or even to go out and enjoy herself. After all the slave is not going anywhere; he will be as She left him on her return.

(See also: bondage, chains, confinement in a car boot, cupboards, dungeon, isolation, overnight sessions, predicament bondage, sensory deprivation, training)

C is for candles

Candles produce a flickering light which is different than you can get with electric lights. They can be perfumed to give a smell that permeates the whole room. Candlelight is both intimate and romantic and also slightly scary with the shadows cast by the candle standing out from the gloom. All of this adds atmosphere to a room when you are playing and intensifies the experience for both Mistress and slave.

But candles are made of wax and as they burn the wax turns liquid. This hot and liquid wax can be dripped upon the tender parts of a slave who is secured so he cannot move. He may be unable to see what is happening in a blindfold or hood and does not know when or where the next drop may fall. This is particularly effective if the wax is being dropped on the balls or nipples.

There are risks using candle wax and it is best to use wax candles that burn at a low temperature not ones that will burn. Check the temperature of the wax with a fingertip before pouring it. Candles that are scented often burn hotter and the liquid wax is too hot and can burn the slave. In any case if the wax is dripped on the slave from a height it will cool a little as it falls and reduce the risk of damage.

i love sessions where Mistress has the lights off and the only light is from candles, in a warm room with a fire keeping us comfortable. But i also enjoy the sudden heat as candle wax is dripped on my nipples and tender parts when i least expect it. Getting the wax off later can be difficult and pulling it off hairs which hold it can be almost as painful as the wax being applied from the candle.

(See also: CBT, nipples, wax, torment and torture)

C is for CBT

CBT stands for cock and ball torture, and applies to anything that is done to torment the slave through action in that area. The penis and balls are full of nerve endings so there is always a lot of sensation from both penis and balls; there are almost as many nerve endings here as around the mouth; it is all so sensitive. So torment can be simple, locking the penis away in a chastity device, or with the parts exposed applying various torments to stimulate. The parts can be crushed, even under the foot of Mistress or even her heel, or squeezed until the slave is shaking and begging for mercy with the pain. Clamps and pegs can be applied to stretch the skin and cause discomfort, or weights hung from the balls to stretch them. Heating cream can be applied which make the area feel on fire, or the whole dipped into a bowl of ice to freeze it. Both heat and cold give the same feeling; the slave may not know whether it is heat or cold that is being applied.

Wax can be dripped on the area or the whole area dipped into a bath of liquid paraffin wax alternating with a bowl of ice until the penis and balls disappear into a solid block of hard wax. Electrodes can be applied so the penis and balls can be shocked, and stimulated electrically with an electro-stimulation device, or a shock collar wrapped around the balls so shocks can be given controlled by a remote control from a hundred yards away. Once the cock and balls are exposed they can be slapped, whipped and paddled until they turn a nice red colour, and all of these can be tried in turn. There are so many ways in which Mistress can torment a slave through his cock and balls and She will know what She wants to do.

i have a Mistress who likes to control my cock and balls all the time with a steel chastity device, but also to hang weights on the balls as i crawl around on all fours. She enjoys applying hot wax or turning my parts into a block of solid wax, and likes to grip and twist my balls when i am helpless in bondage. One simple system is to attach a rope or chain to my ankles and my balls, and my balls and my collar so if i try to straighten my legs then it pulls, or if lift my head it pulls in the other direction. Simple bondage to give me a predicament; which way do i want my balls pulled when i move. All of this is fun to her and torment and pleasure to me, and as much of the time when She is tormenting these parts i am kept hooded and in the dark i never know what is coming next. Her riding crop is particularly well suited to striking the tenderised parts and the discomfort by the time She has finished with me is intense.

Her sharpened nails can be used to bring me almost to orgasm just by application to my balls: just so amazing. She has tried so many things over the years so i find it is best just to wait to see what She wants to try next. It has always been safe, with no danger of damage, but it feels as if my parts are being frozen, boiled, crushed, or twisted and stretched just as Mistress wants. Here She is truly in control as She should be in all things. She owns me as Her property so my parts are Hers to play with as She wishes. Fantastic!

(See also: clamps, crop, electrics, humbler, ice, Mistress's nails, predicament bondage, shock collar, wax, weights)

C is for Caning

A bamboo cane is stiff, flexible, and can strike a target with impressive accuracy. A slave who is to be caned can receive stroke after stroke on exactly the same site until the skin is red, bruised and painful. The cane can be applied gently and give only a slight stinging feeling or so hard that the skin is broken and marks are left for days, weeks, or longer.

The cane is an implement of corporal punishment with a long history. It was used in British schools, especially the public schools until very recently and many men of a certain age will have received their first caning whilst at school. They may now seek to be caned by their Mistress as it reminds them of the past. But a thick and vicious heavy cane is used by the authorities in Singapore to punish those who break the law, and this can even include those who drop litter in the street. A bundle of canes tied together becomes a "birch" which was used until recent years in the Isle of Man to punish offenders. So this is a real implement of punishment used by the law across the world, but also within the world of BDSM. Although household items can be used as a paddle to allow a Mistress to punish their slaves there is no doubt of why a Mistress uses a cane. It is either to support plants in Her garden or to beat and punish Her slaves.

i have only a limited experience of being caned, as Mistress tends to prefer a flogger, whip, or series of paddles, but i have certainly felt the effects on my backside. One year ago before i was to fly to the USA to meet Mistress She arranged for me to go to one of her friends who is a specialist with the cane and to be caned before i flew the next day. This left me with a red and striped backside, uncomfortable to sit on and kept me moving in my seat for the whole flight. Mistress has pointed out that is a good way to prevent the slave developing a clot in his legs from the long flight and it certainly kept me thinking of Mistress the whole journey.

After i was found deficient in my cleaning of Mistress's house whilst She was away i was condemned to be beaten and caned as a result. i knew i would not be left with any permanent marks, but as the date has been arranged just before i was away for a week in the USA. i knew the severity would be greater than i had previously received. i had also been warned that i must ensure that there was no hard skin on my feet or the severity of the caning would be much greater. All of this put me into a state of worry for how i would cope, but at least i was gagged so i did not make too much noise, and it was what Mistress wanted so it was what i deserved and allowed me to show my submission to Mistress as i took the beating. It was so hard and the marks stayed for a week. This was punishment not fun, but Mistress had decided it so it happened as She had decreed.

(See also: crop, discipline, flogging, Judgement of the court, paddles, punishment, spanking, tawse, whipping bench.)

C is for cupboard

Not everyone has space for a cage in which to keep their slave or opportunity to purchase or make one to keep their slaves secure. One option is to use a cupboard instead, which can be locked and leave the slave inside. Most houses have a "cupboard under the stairs" where brushes, vacuum cleaners, and various items are stored and there is no reason not to store slaves there as well.

A couple of sturdy ring bolts attached to the wall or floor will allow Mistress to chain up Her slave within the cupboard, so he is doubly secure. It is also possible to create a cage within the cupboard sing a wire mesh covered frame to form a cage door, and which can hang up on the roof of the cupboard and swing down to be locked in place.
This will limit the space taken up by the slave and allow for storage of all the other things that need to be put away. Once the cage door and the cupboard door are locked the slave is out of the way.

If you do not have a cupboard like this then flat-pack furniture can be modified to make a space at the bottom of a wardrobe which is below a fixed shelf, and the slave can be packed away and the front closed off with a door or metal grille.

i have spent a lot of time locked away in cupboards hooded, in chains and with the cupboard door locked securely. Some of the spaces have been very small and i have been forced to crouch or be curled up into a ball. Other times it has been possible to lie fully flat. They have proved effective to keep me secured helpless and out of the way for as long as Mistress wishes.

(See also: bondage, cage, body bag, dungeon, confinement in a car boot, sensory deprivation, overnight sessions, ownership, training)

C is for crop

Those who ride horses often carry a riding crop which is a short staff with a flap of leather on the end to control their horse. Those who drive horses in harness tend to use a longer whip with a single end to flick the horse and make it go faster.

A riding crop purchased from a riding equipment supplier or on line gives an ideal implement for Mistress to use when chastising her slave. It can be used gently or brought down with full force on any part of the slave. If desired the staff can be used as a cane to beat the slave.

The crop usually gives a sharp stinging pain, but it can be used with extreme accuracy to hit the same part again and again and again, and the slave will see its effects. With care it can be used not just on the backside or back but also on more tender parts such as nipples, cock, or balls. It all depends on what the Mistress wants to do, and how hard She wants to hit the slave.

i find that Mistress tends to use the crop on me as part of a whole session of beating and flogging. This gives her yet another implement to use along with Her whips, paddles, and a long heavy plastic ruler.

(See also: cane, discipline, flogging, paddle, punishment, spanking, tawse, whip, whipping bench, wheel)

C is for confinement in a car boot

Most cars have a boot or trunk to use for carrying luggage and it is usually well ventilated from the rest of the car. Even if there is a separate boot space the back seats often can be pulled down to increase the load space so this means that there is good ventilation.

This means that a Mistress can decide to transport her slave in this space. The slave can be hooded and kept in the dark, and manacled or tied up so he can move very little. He needs to keep quiet if the car is stopped and the Mistress leaves him. He is safe there but has no idea where he is going. This can be used in "kidnap scenarios" where the slave is grabbed and hustled into the car and hooded and bound by a Mistress after first agreeing to this before the event.

A slave can also be transported to some place by his Mistress where She is going to do things to him, either a professional dungeon chamber She has booked or even a friend's house. The main danger comes when the slave is being placed in the boot or taken out, and that comes from bystanders thinking that this is a real kidnap or someone taken away without agreement, so the movement into and out of the car needs to be done somewhere discreet and not overlooked. A Mistress transporting a slave does not want to find herself followed and stopped by the police. Similarly the Mistress needs to be very careful in driving and to prevent any accident or too rapid braking which might throw the slave around in the back. It is best to try this activity for a short period first to check the slave is OK and has good ventilation and does not get too claustrophobic before setting off for a one to two hour drive with a slave secured and helpless. Most slaves can still hear the voice of Mistress and as the slave should not be gagged they can indicate if there is a real problem.

Mistress enjoys having me locked in the boot of her car, leaving me to go to the shops or putting the car through the car wash, and i have been transported hooded and in the dark on a number of occasions for up to a couple of hours when we have been going to stay somewhere. i have had no idea on where we were going, and Mistress has full control

See also: bondage, cage, cupboard, dungeon, isolation, kidnapping, sensory deprivation, travel)

C is for Cuffs

Cuffs usually go around the wrists or ankles and fit tightly to allow a slave to be secured. Other straps around the thighs are sometimes called thigh cuffs, and a cuff can also be fixed around the balls or cock and balls as part of a chastity device.

Cuffs come in a wide range of shapes and sizes, but all are a strip or ring of material which can be secured around the limb, and will not pull off. They have rings and clips attached so the slave can be secured in the position of choice of his Mistress.

Some cuffs are comfortable and padded, others are hard and rough on the skin but for cuffs to be worn for hours or even days they need to be smooth and possibly padded otherwise they can damage the skin and cause sores. The best types of cuffs are inescapable, whether made of steel or with a lock which cannot be opened.

Steel handcuffs can secure the wrists, and there are similar cuffs for the ankles. Both are often linked by chain or a short bar to reduce the slave's movement. Thumb cuffs are small and easily fit into a handbag so are easy to apply to a slave and immobilize him as it is not possible to do much with the thumbs tied together either in front or behind.

Heavy steel cuffs which are lockable are often called manacles, after the term applied to the way in which convicts and prisoners were secured in the past. Some of these can be very heavy so a slave held in manacles can neither escape nor move easily, especially if the manacles can be attached to a heavy collar or via a chain to a fixed wall mounting. Special cuffs for the ankles are part of any system to suspend the slave upside down, secure so he will not slip.

Cuffs can also be used in combination with chains, rope, or other straps to secure a slave to a specific point, or to a cross, frame or rack, or just to make sure he is hobbled and cannot walk around.

My Mistress likes to have me work in heavy steel manacles when i do domestic service. They make it difficult to move around and make the tasks more difficult and also make a clanking sound as i move around. Sometimes i am put in these heavy cuffs and they are used to secure me in the cupboard or in a cage or the back of the car. Other times She allows me lockable leather or rubber cuffs. But whatever she uses it is always secure, and a cuffed slave is not going to get away. She holds the key and i am her prisoner and slave. There is no release from Her cuffs until Mistress decides

(See also: bondage, cupboard, cage, chains, dungeon, leather, predicament bondage, restraint, rope, rubber, rack, suspension)

C is for Chains

Chains for bondage are made of steel, hard, unbreakable and secured with locks to make a slave helpless. They can be used to link cuffs, and allow some movement or to prevent any movement. They are the archetypal method of securing a slave.

But they are heavy to transport, difficult to use in public, and clank when the slave moves. Of course Mistress may like to hear the clank of his chains as a slave does the housework.

Another use of chains is to show that the slave is in bondage in a more symbolic manner. A slave can wear a chain bracelet around each wrist, or ankle chains purchased from a jeweller but locked all the same. He may have a chain around his neck carrying an identity disk that shows he is a slave. These can be worn outside and 24/7 as many would take them as no more than a fashion statement and a bangle. But the Mistress and the slave know better.

Mistress likes me in ankle chains all the time possible, hidden under my socks, and when we are out in public chains around each wrist as well. i wear a chain collar carrying a disk with Mistress's initials on it but this is hidden as well. When i am with Her She likes me in heavy manacles and at night i am often locked away in chains as well as put in the cupboard.

(See also: bondage, cage, cuffs, cupboard, dungeon, leg irons, manacles, overnight sessions, restraint)

C is for corsets and other compressive clothing

During the 19th and early 20th century it was normal for most women to wear a corset, tight around the middle to reduce the size of their waist. Some women wore corsets so tight that the waist size dropped to well below 20 inches. These garments permanently changed the woman's shape, and pressed so hard on the internal organs that it was difficult to breathe. More recently corsets have been worn more for fun, and often outside other clothing as a part of fashion, but they have still had the effect of constricting the woman's waist and making Her look thinner. Elastane and other elastic materials have been used to have the same effect of body shaping and slimming. There are tights to make the legs look slimmer, pants to create the outline of a firm behind, and high-waisted garments to act more like a corset. But those are all designed for women to wear and to suffer the feeling of being crushed by their clothing. There is no reason, however, for a male slave not to feel the same.

Mistress can decide to place the slave in any form of compressive clothing. He can be made to wear tights under his trousers, or put into compression pants or high pants which cover the whole stomach. There are even suppliers of tight elastane pants and vests for the man (Spanx). Part of this can be a direct desire to control the slave, or to humiliate him by making him wear female attire. Part of it is a decision by the Mistress to take control over all of the slave's body, and to make sure he is squeezed and compressed. Part of it is that a man wearing these things is in no doubt who controls him and it helps to remind him that he is a slave all the time not just when he is with his Mistress. Another advantage for the Mistress is that it is difficult for the man to eat much when his stomach is being pressed in, and this helps with weight loss regimes. These things can be worn at work and keep the slave focussed even when working. Some Mistress's like to place their slaves in a corset to increase the pressure on them. The corset is strapped tightly into position and laced tight, and this is a form of bondage. A chain can be locked around the outside to prevent the corset being loosened. It can also be another part of forcing the slave into a feminized state.

i was introduced to constrictive clothing after i reported on wearing anti embolism stockings for a long flight. They squeeze the legs and prevent clots forming, but they are very tight. Mistress immediately decided to place me in support tights under my clothes, and chose ones that were deliberately small for me to increase the pressure. Then came Spanx for pants and tights and a very tight vest designed for men. i wear garments which come up to the top of my stomach and increase the pressure further. i get breathless running up stairs and i feel i am always crushed, but they are warm and it has been a cold winter so Mistress is keeping me controlled, squeezed and warm. Next She introduced me to a corset reducing my waist by a couple of inches. This proved only moderately tight so it was modified to make it even more rigid and tighter. What will come next; will it be an even tighter corset?

(See also: bondage, forced feminization, food control, pressure, spanx, training)

C is for clamps

There are lots of clamps on the market, designed to squeeze things together and which can be used on slaves and applied to their balls, penis and nipples.

Pegs are used to hang up the washing, but applied to the tender parts they are tight and painful, and can be pulled off to give even more pain as the blood gets back into the clamped area. A whole collection of pegs can be threaded on a cord, and pulled of all in one go and this is called a "zipper". Paper clips and clips used to hold papers together can be used for play and are often more severe than the things you can get from adult suppliers.

Clamps can be used for playing with nipples, but a clip attached to the nipple, or a gate clamp kept tight all day allow the nipple to swell and become larger and larger over time. This means the clamps are good to train nipples and make it easier to do more with them. Clamps can be applied to the nipples or balls and be themselves connected by a short chain. This can be used as a lead, or weights can be hung on the clamps to stretch things. The heavier the weight; the greater is the stretch.

Clamps can also be applied to any folds of skin, the mouth, nose or ears and wherever they are placed they are effective in applying pressure. i wear clamps on my nipples all day each day to keep the nipples large and tender for Mistress to play with. She applies clamps where She wants and watches me squirm as the pressure bites.

(See also: bondage, CBT, nipples, torture, zipper)

C is for Consent

i am a slave and i consent freely to everything that my Mistress does to me and with my body. This is essential to any life as a slave. It is a life fully and voluntarily entered into by the slave. he consents every time anything happens. Usually this consent is implicit. The Mistress and slave may have discussed some activity and both have agreed they want to try it. The slave knows what he is giving consent to and both Mistress and slave understand the risks involved. When it happens the slave has already consented, but by going forward he consents again by his actions. If he refused then the Mistress is operating without his consent and this is wrong. It can even be seen as an assault.

There are situations where the law will not accept this type of consent and both the person doing the action and the person receiving it will be in danger of prosecution. This occurs when there is real and actual damage to the slave, when it is taken that there has been actual bodily harm. The law says that no one can consent to this. One example of this type of behaviour is where a slave is branded at his request by his Mistress. In the United Kingdom this is a crime, but it is not so in all countries, which is why branding of UK slaves tends to occur outside the UK.

If there is going to be a prolonged session it may be wise for there to be a semi-formal Form of Consent by the slave to show the Mistress that he is really prepared for what is going to happen. The formal slave contract will cover most areas of activity and allow both the Mistress and the slave to agree and sign to show their consent. Even here this is not a legally enforceable contract but it does have immense psychological power to show the slave his situation and to spell out the power to be enjoyed by the Mistress

Consent is the basis of everything that happens in a Mistress /slave relationship, as it should be in the rest of life as well.

Here is an example of a detailed Form of Consent covering a specific period when bondage and torment for the slave were likely to be intense and prolonged

FORM OF CONSENT

I, the slave ......,... slave of the Most High and Exalted Mistress, Mistress .... do hand myself over completely to her control for a 24 hour period starting at 5pm on the 6th of February 2008.

I realise that I will be kept all of the time in some level of bondage, including wearing my collar for the whole 24 hours and that I may be secured in any bondage, including cuffs, rope, chains, handcuffs and leg irons, or any other method my Mistress may wish to use on me

I consent to

this

I realise that I may be moved anywhere for bondage, beaten and torment at the decision of my Mistress, and may be carried bound, gagged and blindfolded in the boot of a car so that I will not know where I am going

I consent to

this

I realise that I may be tormented in any way my Mistress may decide, including severe nipple torment, hot wax, for which I shall be providing extra candles, electrics, CBT and that I will be beaten repeatedly with all implements at the disposal of my Mistress

I consent to

this

I realise that I will be left overnight in bondage in cuffs and chains, CB3000 and dildo, with my hands bund up with bondage tape and I will remain there until my Mistress decides to release me my time may be made more difficult by application of heating cream to my cock, backside, and on pads strapped to my nipples to keep me warm.

I consent to this

I realise that I will be completely under the control of my Mistress to carry out any tasks she may decide, including to act as her driver, dressed however she may decide. I realise that any failure to carry out any task to her complete satisfaction will be punished severely and without mercy.

I consent to this

I consent to whatever my Mistress may decide to do to me and with my body during the full 24 hours of the session, but will be released after that not permanently damaged but with the marks of my beatings including bruising and the straight lines of the cane.

I consent to this

I realise that my servitude does not end with my release on the Friday but continues in my following life as Her slave.

I consent to this

Signed   the slave

Date
.../.../.....

(See also: bondage, branding, chastity, contracts, domination, flogging, ownership, overnight sessions, power, submission)

C is for Contract

A contract is an agreement between two or more people. It tends to be drawn up in a format which owes much to legal documentation even when it is not an enforceable legal act. Contracts are used to define the role of the slave and his Mistress in a relationship and the expectations that each may have of the other. A contract may cover a specific topic or be more general and cover all areas of a slave's life and the behaviour expected of him.

Male chastity often makes use of a chastity contract to make everything clear before the man is locked in the chastity device under the control of his key-holder. The signing of the chastity contract is an important step which takes the wearer of a male chastity device into a new world of prolonged control and chastity and this is made clear in the contract. i have included a chastity contract in the section on chastity. Other chastity contracts can be found in "Restart Intimacy "by Sierra Parker, other books on male chastity and on the internet.

Slave contracts cover so much more than chastity. They can be explicit and cover all areas of a slave's life so everything is clearly spelled out, or they can be short and have little detail. The shortest chastity contract i have seen was very simple:

Contract of Slavery

The slave…………… to be know under his new name of
…………… agrees to be the slave of the Mistress ………………..

He gives control of his life over to Her. From the signature of this contract She will be in control of all areas of his life both at home and outside. Although he may make suggestions and discuss issues with his Mistress She will decide. he freely grants all power to the Mistress.

This contract will run for 12 months and may be renewed.

Signed   the slave

Signed   the Mistress

Dated   …./…./…..

Which can be summarized as "slave and Mistress may discuss, but She decides".

One advantage of using more complex contracts of slavery is that it makes clear the Mistress's expectations for Her slave. It may look quite shocking to a slave when he is first given a slave contract to read, but he will know what he is letting himself in for. There can also be negotiation over specific points before a final version is ready. But once the contract is signed then the slave must realise that he must submit to the terms of the contract and be ready to obey his Mistress.

One problem of contracts is that often they look good, and might look as if they could apply to every area of a slave's life but it may not be possible to enforce the contract. The slave may have outside commitments including work which cannot be ducked and this should be allowed for in the contract. If the slave is married and his Mistress is not his wife then this will limit what can be covered and the powers of the Mistress. Contracts need to be grounded in the reality of the situation not the fantasy and desire of the slave and his Mistress. If the contract is not so grounded then it will fail.

One situation where contracts do not apply is where a slave has passed into the state of being the property and not just the slave of his Mistress. Here the slave is not free to sign a contract as he is fully owned by his Mistress. Of course this is not legally enforceable but it feels like it and is a development of the slave state. In this situation instead of a yearly review of the slave contract between Mistress and slave it is best to have a similar discussion leading to the production of a "Memorandum of Understanding " to define the roles of Mistress and slave.

From the internet and from books one might think that once a slave contract is signed then everything is decided for good. But this is rarely the case so it is best to have a defined time for the contract and then to look again at what should be in it as new circumstances demand. A year contract is probably too long for a starter contract which should be for only a few months, but once established a year contract with automatic review does seem to work. My experience as a slave is that i was permitted to have a slave contract after being first enslaved by Mistress on my first meeting with Her, then accepted as a slave, then only after several months when she knew me in greater detail did She consent to the use of a slave contract. This grew into a yearly contract reviewed and signed each November. But two years ago it all changed after I had been a slave for four years when She decided that i had become Her property. Now there are no more contracts but a yearly discussion and a "Memorandum of Understanding". There is no doubt She owns me as property, and seeks to develop me further to improve my skills and attention to Her.

Here is a more detailed slave contract which can be used once Mistress and slave have decided what need to be there. It is simply a template and sections can be retained or deleted. It all depends on what both want. The contract covers all sorts of issues, from the simple and practical to the more complicated. It can be used to build your own contract that reflects your situation.

Once a Mistress and slave have discussed the contract it needs to be drawn up, checked and then be ready for signing. This is a big moment as the slave is formally giving up power to his Mistress and she is accepting that power and responsibility. Sometimes the signing ceremony can be carried out in the presence of witnesses who are friends of the Mistress and slave and who know their situation. It can also incorporate a formal collaring ceremony when the slave is collared and starts to wear the collar his Mistress has brought for him to show he is slave to Her alone.

CONTRACT OF SLAVERY

Between Mistress………….. and

The slave …………………..

Signed at   On the……..day of
……..2013

  This contract freely entered into by both parties shall take effect
immediately on signing, and shall last for   in the
first instance. The contract shall be binding upon the slave except
if there are major medical issues which prevent him carrying out
his duties. Mistress can bring the contract to an end at any time if
there is unacceptable behaviour by the slave or factors that prevent
Her controlling him adequately. The slave can be transferred to
another Mistress if Mistress decides to do so.

Names
The slave will address Mistress ……… as Mistress both in private and in public except
when Mistress decides otherwise, which may occur from time to time in public when
they are with persons who might not understand. The slave can be called by any name
Mistress decides, and She has the power to change his name and designation at any time.

Mistress's Obligations
The Mistress will ensure the safety of Her slave and provide for him basic levels of care
and support. She will work to develop him as her slave. She always has the right to have
her desires fulfilled by the slave except when it might cause him actual permanent harm
or damage or put him at risk of this.

Slave Obligations
The slave has an obligation to obey all orders of his Mistress both in private and in
public. he must question an order if he does not understand it and must strive at his
utmost to carry out all tasks that are given to him and show proper respect to his Mistress
at all times. he is Her slave.

Communication
The slave is required to inform his Mistress if there are any problems in carrying out any
order that prevent it being carried out. He shall make himself available to talk by phone,

to text and to communicate by Skype when it is convenient to his Mistress. The Mistress shall communicate with Her property when it is convenient for Her to do so, and may only be able to do so at limited times of which she will inform Her slave. If She is busy when the slave telephones he will not be allowed to speak. The slave must text Mistress before speaking to check that She is free to talk.

Finances

The slave shall be expected to provide the sum of £   to Mistress at the beginning of this period of slavery as a deposit to be held by her to ensure his good behaviour and as his tribute to Her. The deposit shall be forfeit if there is any unacceptable behaviour by the slave. She will also require regular tributes which will depend on whether he is attending her or whether communication is via Skype, text, and email only.

Service

The slave owes service to his Mistress. This is the service that SHE requires of him, and he must not approach Her, or contact Her without Her permission. He is NOT to bother Her with frequent calls or texts or emails, but is to wait to be contacted. He will be given the opportunity to serve Her in many different ways, which She will decide. Outside of those times when he is permitted to be with Her this will include obtaining items that She requires or desires.

When he is allowed to attend Her he will be dressed as SHE decides and must always appear well groomed and clean. he will be expected to carry out tasks immediately on receiving an order, and he will be judged by what he does, not what he says. Mistress may choose to use her voice and words or tone of speech to encourage him, but She will decide at all times how she speaks to him and treats him. The slave will be expected to carry out regular domestic duties for his Mistress.

Etiquette

The slave must always be polite and show respect to his Mistress as his Superior, be clean and without odour, well shaved and well groomed. he must never be under the influence of drink or drugs.

Chastity

The slave will be required to be chaste with no masturbation at all and will be locked into a chastity device which he will provide. Mistress will decide on how the key-holding is to be managed and may require the slave to have his device locked with a plastic lock which may not be removed without her permission. The slave must be prepared at any time to show that he is locked away and that the lock has not been tampered with. This will allow for the slave to be released if there are specific medical issues that require the device to be removed.

Punishment

The slave will be punished by his Mistress for any acts of wilful disobedience. Mistress will sentence him to such punishment as She will decide appropriate and right. There is no appeal.

Rituals, Protocols and Rules

The slave shall always address his Mistress as Mistress, except when she decides otherwise. On arrival into her presence he shall immediately kneel at her feet to kiss Her shoes or feet and remain there until permitted to rise. This shall occur both in private and in public. When the slave is dismissed from the presence of his Mistress he shall kneel to kiss Her feet before he leaves and shall stay in that position until allowed to rise. Mistress may permit the slave not to do this in public if SHE chooses.

All other rules and protocols shall be decided by the Mistress. She has the final decision in all that occurs with slave and is under no obligation to accede to any of his wishes unless She wishes to do so.

Appendix 1
Mistress requires that the slave have the hair removed from his penis, balls and crack. He is to have this area waxed regularly and will be inspected to check that this has been carried out

Summary

The slave……………. has agreed to become the slave of Mistress ……….and to submit to Her will and control and to obey Her and serve Her. He will be kept in chastity. Wilful failure in obedience will lead to punishment and the slave can be dismissed for any behaviour deemed unacceptable by the Mistress.

Signed   **The Mistress**

Signed   **the slave**

Date

Date of review of slave contract:

C is for Collar

i am a slave and i wear a steel collar around my neck engraved
with my Mistress's name, my slave name, and the date i was
collared. It shows that i am a slave and belong to Mistress.
Although it is quite broad it fits easily around my neck and is
invisible under my shirt and tie in public. No one can see i am a
slave unless my shirt is undone, but i know that is my state.

A collar on a slave signifies that he is a slave. A lead can be
attached and he can be pulled around on the end of the lead. The
collar can have a chain attached which can be used to secure the
slave by his neck. He knows that the collar shows his state.

Collars come in all sorts of different shapes and sizes from the
heavy steel collar weighing 500-1000 gm which weighs down the
slave and can be part of a set of manacles and leg irons to
something much smaller and lighter. Collars can be made of
rubber, leather, and steel, and plain or embellished with the
Mistress's name as owner.

When a slave starts training he may be introduced to a collar to
wear during training sessions at first, then for longer and longer
periods until he is wearing it 24/7.

Miss Abernethy in her groundbreaking book "Erotic Slave-hood"
talks of her preference of having a slave in a locked collar, and I
can see her point. The click of the lock as the collar is secured
marks the point at which a person accepts slave-hood, and being
the slave and property of another. It is a physical act, and an
immensely symbolic action and underpins the state of the slave and
his Mistress

Once a slave has accepted he is to wear a collar then Mistress needs to decide the type of collar She prefers. There are times when a locked collar may not be easily worn but a chain necklace can be easily purchased from jewellery shops and the clasp glued shut. The slave is now in a chain collar which looks as if it is simply a piece of jewellery but he knows better. Collars need to be removed to go through airport style security but the collar can always be put back on once the security has been passed.

The slave may be required to provide a collar to wear for his Mistress and also to obtain a dog-tag to show his slave name and that of his Mistress to attach to it
Few Mistresses require the collar to be visible in public, but occasionally someone who is wearing an obvious collar can be seen.

Once going for a walk i was passed by a couple out walking hand in hand. As i passed i realised that the woman was wearing a leather collar, and looking around i noticed that it was secured by a padlock at the back. No one seemed to have noticed anything, and i only noticed because i was wearing a collar locked around my neck under my shirt collar and hidden at the same time. She had the nerve to be out in public in her collar; mine was hidden and invisible.

At some point in the life of a slave his Mistress may decide that the time has come for him to be "collared" formally. This is a big step and the click of the lock on the collar as it is attached is one of those moments when a slave's whole world changes.
The acceptance of a collar by a slave means that he is accepting fully that he is the slave of his Mistress. The provision of a collar

that the Mistress has selected, purchased, and had marked with her slave's name, shows that She accepts him fully as Her slave.

The application of the collar can be a simple act, or can be worked into a more elaborate ceremony, sometimes with witnesses and friends present to celebrate the collaring. The slave kneels there, eyes shut or blindfolded, and Mistress applies the collar and secures it in place. The slave is collared; later he is allowed to see himself in a mirror to see what has been done. When Mistress applied the steel collar she had bought for me i had no idea of what type of collar She had selected, and it was only when She lead me to a mirror that i could see the collar in place, a steel band around my neck. She says that when i saw it i gasped and my eyes went wide with shock. It looks good around my neck and shows She is Mistress and i am slave.

There is such a feeling of freedom in a strange way when i am put into a locked collar. Any of my past worries disappear, and i become focussed on the fact that i am Her slave and property and there to submit and obey Mistress alone.

(See also: bondage, bondage at work, consent, contract, domination, ownership, submission, training)

D is for Domination

A Mistress dominates her slave; a slave submits to the dominance and authority of his Mistress. This is a relationship in which there is a transfer of power from the man to the Mistress. The man willingly agrees to give power to his Mistress and to consent to Her having the power over him. The Mistress agrees to take possession of the slave as a slave and to have control over him. All of this is openly agreed and the slave consents to it fully.

If the domination is not with consent then it is an application of force and is wrong. Of course once the slave has consented to be under the control of his Mistress she will exercise Her power over him and it is his duty to submit and obey.

Some people are naturally dominant, and dominate the space around them by their appearance, body language, and how they speak. This is a part of "command presence" which is needed when one is to command and others need to follow. It can be learned but some people are better at it than others. Some women just look so powerful, dressed to impress, standing tall, radiating an aura of power. Such people do well in business and in life.

Others of us have an outward dominant personality, which we may need for work, but inside we are drawn more to be the one who is dominated, and wish to be submissive and learn to obey. The two personality types can be present in the same person, who may need to be powerful in one situation but the opposite in private. Many slaves are of this type, which draws them to the presence of powerful Women and Mistresses and leads them into a life of slavery to a powerful Mistress.

Although the Mistress can emphasise her power by the way She dresses and stands, and the attitude She takes in speaking to her slaves it is Her innate power that shines through. Mistress has such a strong personality, but it is Her total power which She expresses just be standing there, or even at rest sitting in splendour which acts like an electric shock on me and causes me to drop to my knees and prostrate myself.

Others might not notice it, but i am drawn to my ever so Dominant Mistress because She is whom She is, but also because i have such a strong desire to be dominated, and to submit. She saw this in me the first time we met. Dominance sees its opposite in those of us who desire to submit, which is why the duality of domination and fully consensual submission gives the whole dynamic to the relationship.

i truly desire to submit and my Mistress knows it and i know she accepts my desire and so this builds her power and dominance over me. This is not just when i am with her, though the sense of her power over me when i attend her is almost palpable, but it allows her to know that She will give me orders and that they will be carried out. She wants something obtained, or a task carried out. i will do it, and with each task and opportunity for Her to show her dominance the bond grows stronger.

From time to time i realise that i have been given an order, carried it out, and not even thought about it. This could be that Mistress has ordered me to eat specific food for lunch each day. She ordered it so i do it.

The innate and learned skills of domination that are shown by Mistress allow her to control me, to train me, and to change me as She decides. Her power radiates from her and in her presence i am loath to say anything other than "Yes Mistress" to whatever the order. Her dominance is paramount in everything i do with Her and for Her

Domination of the slave by his Mistress who takes control over him, and submission by the slave who is there to obey Mistress are at the core of what it is to be a slave.

(See also: collar, consent, contract, food control, exercise, ownership, power exchange, reality, submission, training,)

D is for Dungeon

The picture that comes to mind when the word dungeon is used is of a dark, dank cell is which a slave is kept indefinitely. Alternatively it is a space filled with apparatus for torture, racks, frames for whipping, cages, with rows of whips on the wall and cupboards full of toys. This is the "red room of pain" belonging to Christian Grey in the 50 Shades of Grey Trilogy.

Professional Mistresses tend to work from premises which have some of this dungeon apparatus in a room where they can dominate and torment the men who come as clients. But this is not what happens for most slaves and their Mistresses. There are few free rooms or cellars in the average house.

Most slaves receive their whipping and are cast into bondage in the bedroom or living room at home. Perhaps there maybe a ringbolt on the wall in one corner to which the slave can be attached. Even here a cupboard can be modified to produce a "holding cell". i once modified a cupboard under the stairs for Mistress with a cage built into it and rows of hooks on which to hang Her whips and toys. It was perhaps the "smallest dungeon in the world" with a cage 3ft x 3ft with a sloping ceiling, and a total size of 6ft x 3ft. Even then most activity occurred elsewhere in the house.

Any place a Mistress designates as Her dungeon is a dungeon, no matter how much or how little equipment is there. She decides what She calls any space in Her house or flat. Some Mistresses take their slaves out to parties of like minded individuals. Here the premises often have stocks, racks, or other equipment with which the participants can play.

But there are also dungeons for hire, in the UK, USA, and all over the world. These are fully equipped play spaces usually with a bedroom and bathroom as well and can be hired by the hour or longer. It is possible to find them via the internet via a search for dungeons for hire or something similar. Mistress and slave can use them for a "holiday" or even a weekend away. Many cost little more than the cost of a good hotel room for the same period. This gives Mistress a chance to play with a wider range of equipment.

my experiences started visiting Professional Mistresses in their chambers but now for many years i have been slave to a Most Powerful Mistress and we have used whatever is available to us with occasional trips away to dungeon spaces for a night or weekend visit. Playing away from home like this in a dungeon often shows Mistress things She likes and then gets to use on me. Then we get them to use again.

(See also: bondage, cage, cupboard, travel, training, overnight sessions)

D is for Domestic service

There are no tasks around the home which cannot be carried out by a slave. But the problem is that most male slaves are not competent to carry out such tasks and need a period of training. Different Mistresses like different tasks performed for them but all know They want any work done to a high standard.

So a slave needs to be trained, supervised and assessed. He needs to learn to clean and polish, to clean a bathroom, kitchen, or indeed all rooms. He will need to be checked as he does this and if his work is not up to standard then he may need to do the job again and be punished as well. Slaves can be allowed to do the work in their own clothes or required to wear the uniform that Mistress decides. This may be a simple "livery" or they may be made to dress in female clothes as a maid. There is no reason why they cannot be required to do the work wearing restraints or manacles and a "dog shock collar" around the balls can be used to shock them if the work is being done too slowly.

Domestic service can be used for so many tasks that a Mistress would otherwise have to do herself. Slaves can be sent out to do the shopping from a list and to put it away. They can be required to clean a whole house then set to wash the car and do the gardening.

Mistress may expect her slave to make and serve drinks to both Her and Her friends. he can be trained to provide meals and expected to do the washing up and put away afterwards. Any slave who craves a beating or any other torment can be denied it until his tasks are completed.

All of these things are there for the slave to do and he must submit and obey his Mistress. Mistress does need to be ready to supervise, to praise (rarely) if a task has been completed to Her satisfaction and to arrange training so a slave becomes skilled in performing the domestic service. There are a wide range of books, on line resources and courses available.

Domestic service can include making the beds, taking out the trash and doing the laundry. The slave can be taught to wash, dry, iron, and put away to Mistress's satisfaction. All Her boots and shoes may need polishing and putting tidily away.
There are almost no limits to the range of tasks in domestic service a slave can be given to do. It can remove boring tasks from a Mistress and give Her more time to enjoy Herself.

When a slave and Mistress live together a system can be established where the man takes over more and more of the domestic tasks so he can provide domestic service for his Mistress and both will gain. She will have a nice clean house and be less tired; he will be serving Her.

my list of domestic tasks varies. Mistress decides the tasks She wants performed, the way, the standard, and the penalty for failure. But i have found a deep satisfaction in carrying out tasks of domestic service as a slave knowing my place is to serve.

(See also: contracts, discipline, female supremacy, female lead relationship, manacles, personal service, training, shock collar, submission, uniform, work, zapped)

D is for Discipline

Discipline is a word with multiple meanings. It can be used to describe the process of punishing or disciplining a slave. Here the discipline is what the Mistress applies to Her slave; he needs to be disciplined.

Discipline can be applied in many different ways. The slave can receive a beating or whipping, or be put into solitary confinement or made to stand in the corner. This discipline shows the power the Mistress has over Her slave. In some relationships there is a weekly discipline meeting when the failures of the slave over the week are added up and the relevant level of punishment decided and given. The slave is held under the disciplinary rule of his Mistress and She wields the discipline. It is a bit like an old style school where the teachers controlled discipline and caned pupils whom they decided needed it.

But there is also the discipline of being a slave. The practice of living by the rules and orders of a Mistress requires that the slave develops self discipline to make sure everything is done properly. The slave may only be with Mistress some of the time. She needs to know that he will act according to Her orders and rules for eating, drinking, internet use etc. This is no different than the discipline that children develop which means they brush their teeth, wash their hands and make sure their trousers are properly done up.

In military life discipline is key to getting troops to work together and act in a disciplined manner automatically. It is the same process for a slave; he needs to develop the practices his Mistress requires so they come automatically. He needs to learn how to greet Her, how to serve Her, when She wants him silent and how She wants him to behave in company. She may require him to be Her driver and he needs to prepare the car, open the doors for Her, and get her to her destination on time.

So a slave lives his life under the discipline of his Mistress, trained to the self discipline required for service as She desires and is disciplined by Her when he falls short of her standards.

(See also: contracts, domestic service, punishment, training)

D is for Disorientation and Darkness

When i am placed in a heavy hood i cannot see. If my hearing is compromised by earplugs and external sounds i lose the ability to hear as well. Put away in darkness i have no idea of how long i have been there.

If i am moved around in a hood, or transported in the boot of a car hooded and shackled i have no idea of where i am being taken.

The darkness presses down upon me and makes other senses go into overdrive. A touch, the sound of Mistress's voice, Her perfume all become so powerful. i am helpless in the dark and i feel vulnerable, as everything feels so much more sensitive. If i am beaten in the dark i have no idea of when or how the next blow will fall. If hot wax is dripped on my nipples it feels so hot and sudden as it touches the skin even if this is not so, because all my senses are heightened.

So darkness intensifies sensation as anyone who has ever worn a blindfold will know. Long periods of darkness have the effect of disorientating the victim as well. If i wake in the night in bondage and hood i wake not knowing where i am or what is happening and it takes a few moments to remember where i am and that all is OK. Darkness can even cause panic even when i know that all is safe.

But when the hood is removed and i emerge blinking into the light i am disorientated. i do not always know where i am or what is happening. This is particularly true if i have been transported to somewhere by car but even a night in darkness leaves me disorientated until i see the face of Mistress and know fully where i am.

Darkness and disorientation are used to stress captives, kidnapped or taken for interrogation. The darkness intensifies all their experiences and everything that is done to them seems so much more threatening. Long periods in darkness leave the subject confused and disorientated so less able to withstand interrogation. These techniques can be used by a Mistress on her slave.

The effect is to leave the slave vulnerable and the sight of Mistress reminds them of the outside world and that She is there. It also shows Her control over the slave. It is Mistress who decides when a slave is allowed to see or hear. She controls this and everything else as well.

(See also: blindfold, cage, dungeon, cupboard, hood, isolation, kidnap, military, overnight sessions, sensory deprivation, travel,)

D is for Dildo

A dildo is a device designed to be inserted into a person. Many are penis shaped and designed to be placed in the female vagina; but they come in a wide range of sizes and shapes and can be designed to vibrate as well.

A dildo may be used by his Mistress on a male slave. he may be forced to take it into his mouth to emphasis Her power over him, or it may be pushed inside his anus. The dildo can be applied gently stretching things to push it inside or roughly forcing an entrance. The slave is there to submit to this and to allow his Mistress access to all parts of him. She decides the nature and size of the device, its shape and whether it is able to vibrate or designed to give electric shocks.

Some devices are designed to stay inside for long periods and these tend to be called butt plugs. Some have attachments so they can be attached to some other form of external bondage. Some have electrodes to allow Mistress to shock Her slave.

Some Mistresses wear a strap on device with a protruding dildo attached to a harness worn by Her and use it on their slaves. She can use this as a surrogate penis to penetrate Her slave and show her total power over him and his helplessness.

The use of a dildo on a male slave emphasises the fact that all of them is under the control of Mistress including their arse, and that She is showing Her power by what She does. It is in some ways the ultimate humiliation and evidence that the slave belongs to another. Some Mistresses require their slave to clean out their bowels before a dildo is applied and have an enema. Then the slave is cleaned out and afterwards is ready for penetration.

Dildos can be made of a wide variety of materials hard or soft, inflatable or metal but all are there to penetrate into the slave at the whim of his Mistress.

(See also: arse, butt plugs, electrics, enemas, humiliation, strap on, submission)

E is for electrics

Nerves carry very small electrical impulses from the brain to the muscles to make them contract, and from the skin and other sensory areas to the brain to allow us to feel things.

Electrical stimulation of nerves can be used to make muscles twitch and tone them up, (Slendertone devices) or to give extra sensation from the very mild to the most severe. If mains electricity is used this electrocutes and causes the heart to stop causing death, so direct AC mains electricity should never be used on a slave.
Electrical stimulation above the waist is also a potential problem as it can affect the heart electrical activity as well and cause abnormal heart rhythms.

But that still leaves lots of places where electrical stimulation can be used to increase sensation. Electrodes attached to the skin can cause a burning sensation or a mild buzzing. Harder shocks will make muscles twitch and contract directly. Electrodes placed around the penis or on the balls can be used to intensify pleasant sensations or be so severe they cause the slave to cry out with the pain. Butt plugs can be equipped with electrodes to make the backside twitch and to stimulate the prostrate directly.

Control us usually via a control box powered by batteries so it is always important to have a good supply of spares, and to make sure the electrodes are in good contact with the area desired. If the system does not work then it is usually because the electrodes have become loose.

Some stimulation systems are connected to the electrodes by wires, but others use a remote controller. The Mistress can shock Her slave from across the room or even further away. There are systems (such as the DL2000 from www. Dreamloverlaboratories.com) which can be controlled by computer so a Mistress can watch her slave being shocked on Skype, whilst controlling everything from thousands of miles away. Here the electrodes are built into a chastity device worn by the slave, and a small USB attached to a computer allows the controller to really control Her slave.

One option is to purchase a "dog shock collar". This is a collar which fits around the neck of a dog and has a small shocking device on it which gives sharp shocks to train the dog. The range of the remote is claimed to be up to 400 yards or further. For dogs they are banned in the UK but legal in the USA. For human slaves the collar is wrapped around the balls with the electrode prongs on the skin, but not around the neck where it would be dangerous. Then the mistress can zap the slave whenever She feel She needs or wants to do it.

But not all shocks are unpleasant. A soft repetitive low power stimulus can be very arousing and pleasant like a soft buzzing and shaking. Here the stimulus can be given to give the slave pleasure, though having your balls vibrated and being aroused when you are already locked securely in a chastity device is pleasure but frustration both at the same time.

There are a wide range of electro-stimulation systems available which can stimulate all the tender parts. It is probably worth buying a simple system to begin with a wire to a simple controller. Then if this seems to work and is effective a more expensive system with remote control can be obtained. Some of the systems cost up to $1000 so are very expensive, so starting with simple systems is best.

my experience with electrics came first with a Mistress who liked to insert a butt plug with electrodes and then shock me when i did not expect it. The mild shocks were OK but the most powerful shocks had me in agony and crying out for mercy.

Mistress then used a remote system on me and obtained a DL2000 which She used when She was away to control me from the other side of the world. On one memorable occasion She was shocking me in the UK from a beach in South Africa whilst i could be seen suffering on Skype.

Most recently She has enjoyed the power of the shock collar around my balls especially when we are both out in public and has used a controller with wire connection under the table when we have been in a café having a meal. Being controlled by Mistress is always good, but a severe shock if i forget myself in public nearly brings me to my knees, and shows me again who is my boss.

Perhaps shock control and stimulation might work well to get men to learn new behaviours and lose bad habits; a shock every time he picks his nose will soon make a man lose the bad habit.

(See also chastity, medical, punishment, remote control, shock collar, training, zapped)

E is for Enemas

An enema is a quantity of fluid given up inside the anus of a slave. It fills the bowel, and loosens anything there. Then it is expelled and leaves the bowel empty and ready to use in play. The fluid needs to be neither too hot or too cold and run in steadily so as not to damage the bowel. A couple of pints or a litre and a half can be given but many enemas are much smaller in amount. The more that is put in the harder to hold it in and the greater the need of the slave to get to a toilet so he can empty his bowels. There are systems used by alternative therapists to allow them to irrigate the bowels with larger quantities of fluid and this is termed colonic irrigation where fluid is run in and out to empty the colon.

Enemas are administered medically when the bowel needs to be emptied for an examination, or when the patient is very constipated. They can be used as part of "medical" play.

When a slave is made to place themselves so a nozzle can be inserted into their anus, and they are forced to stay still whilst they are filled and wait for Mistress to allow them to empty themselves it is a major humiliation for the slave. His bodily functions and even whether he becomes incontinent of mess depends on his total obedience and how far his Mistress wants to go. She can put in a couple of pints of fluid so he feels so filled up, then make him wait and hold it all in until he leaks, then punish him for his failure. Men like to be clean and know that their bowels are under control. Anything that takes this away is humiliating, and to be placed in this situation by Mistress really shows Her power.

If a slave is to have a dildo inserted into his rectum or be required to wear a butt plug for a long period some Mistresses require him to have an enema first.

Some Mistresses like to give their slave an enema and some slaves like it as well.

i have been given an enema once many years in the past, and i found it so difficult to keep it all in. i was worried i was going to make a mess and found it very humiliating, more so even than being used as a toilet for Mistress to pass urine into. Lucky for me my Mistress is not into enemas yet.

(See also: arse, butt plugs, dildo, humiliation, medical, strap on, submission)

E is for Exercise

Many men are fat and flabby and have lost any muscle they had when they were young. This is not the sort of slave that most Mistresses want. They want a slave who is fit and has good muscles. he may need to be on all fours for hours as a footstool or seat, and to keep in a single position until Mistress allows movement. He may be needed to carry heavy loads or even to pull a cart with Mistress in it. Mistress wants him fit and will wish him to exercise to get this.

Mistress can give the slave an exercise regime to start to toughen him up. He can be made to practice sit ups and press ups and to stand on his toes. If Mistress is going to make him wear heels he will need to learn to stand tall. Once he is on a regime Mistress can expect him to do it every day and to demonstrate the exercises in front of Her. Once he can do something to Her satisfaction She can increase the load and the number of exercises.

Some slaves can be set to join a gym and to take formal fitness classes, use weights, or to walk to work 3-5 miles a day instead of taking the car. The slave can be made to run on the spot or up and down stairs until he is ready to collapse, and all the time Mistress is doing it for his own good. He can be expected to use the stairs instead of a life at work, even in a 10 storey tower block. Of course there is no reason why Mistress will necessarily want to make things easy for the slave. he may be required always to do his sit ups with a butt plug in place, or stimulated with the electrics if his exercising in front of Her is not as good as She would wish.

She has so many implements to "encourage" the slave, both used when he is exercising for Her and also a punishment if he misses out on his daily exercises or fails to get as fit as She wishes.

The slave can have his food controlled to make sure he is not eating junk food, his fluid intake monitored to make him drink more, and his weight checked to se he is losing weight. Exercise, diet and total weight are all under the control of Mistress. Whatever the slave is doing or wherever he has to go he can be required to stick to Her diet, her exercise regime and to be the weight She wants. This all gives mistress the body She desires on Her slave, a slave fit to serve Her.

Mistress has me on a diet regime, and an exercise regime currently of sit ups and press ups. She inspects me to see i am getting fitter and checks my weight. She controls these areas of my life as much as She does others with chastity, chains and a collar.

(See also: food control, slave as furniture, medical, ownership, pony play)

F is for female supremacy

"Female Supremacy" means that women should have power and dominion over men; men are there to serve women.

In the past men had the power over women and women struggled to get a fair chance in life. But now things have changed. Two of the most powerful leaders in the world are Angela Merkel the Chancellor of Germany, who runs Europe, and Hilary Clinton who was American Secretary of State and might become President.

The law has changed to give equal opportunities in work. More women have a university education and are moving into management and leadership positions.

i have always considered women equal to men but my position has changed. It could be working for a female CEO but i have been slave to a most powerful Mistress for several years as well whom i serve.

Now i feel that Female Supremacy is right for this century. i know that Women are Superior. They can juggle multiple roles, work well in teams and are better organised than most men. My Mistress is superior to me; serving Her feels natural.

Perhaps all power should be given to Women and taken from men and we should move to a "Female Supremacy State".

F is for Female led relationships (FLR)

A female lead relationship is one in which the woman leads and has a degree of control over the man. In the past the man was usually seen as the head of household and in charge, but even then there were lots of households where the woman was in charge because the man was gone or away and some where the women ruled and the men were the followers.

Now with more equality in relationships many couples try to work together with neither of them in charge. This is often frustrating because of problems of communication and so many of these relationships have issues unresolved, rows and trouble.

One way out of this is for the woman to take charge or for the man to agree that there are areas of life in which the woman leads. Both need to discuss issues, but it is agreed in advance that one will make the final decisions. Unless there is good communication between the two this is a recipe for disaster, but with good communication, discussion and agreement this is a model which works well and reduces conflict in the relationship.

Common areas of conflict in relationships are in the areas of how often the couple have sex which can be a problem if one wants it often and the other not so much, money, housework, use of free time, and the direction of development for both of the partners. These are described in web sites such as "aboutFLR" and others concerned with female lead relationships, marriage or households as the 5 food groups and in a female lead relationship the woman takes over control of one or more of these with the full consent of the man.

This is not slavery and the man is not slave to the woman, unless both want it to be like that, but there is a real exchange of power between the couple after full discussion and agreement. FLR contracts can be produced showing what areas are controlled and how, just the same as chastity and slave contracts so the process of discussion and agreement on a contract is much the same.

Sex

Sex is one of the most important areas to discuss and consider. In a typical FLR household the man has agreed to let the women control sex, what they do and how often. They have agreed this in advance, and given it a try before any agreement is made formally. There is still the possibility of discussion of positions and techniques for sexual intercourse, foreplay, and fantasies, but the woman has control of what actually happens. She may want the man to be without orgasm in a chastity agreement, and will typically want him to stop masturbation.

This may mean they need to introduce a chastity device. She may want more oral sex and her partner to do it in the way She wants. She will decide what is done and how often, so there is no more whinging about him wanting sex all the time and Her being too tired, or him not wanting to experiment when She wants to do so. This is a powerful tool to transform the bickering about sex that can damage a relationship to the simple situation where She controls it and everything to do with it.

Housework

In most households the woman does more than Her fair share of housework even if both the man and the woman go out to work. Men often leave their things in a mess and only want to do the things they like, pottering in the garden, playing with DIY etc. In a FLR the situation is different. As the woman now controls the sex the man knows he must please her to get any at all. He responds by wanting to do things for Her. Now is the time for a frank discussion of what needs to be done around the house and for the man to step forward to take his part of the work. This means that in practice he may begin to take over most of the housework.

Many men do like doing things for their partner, and in an FLR relationship they can have full rein to do this with support to help them do it right. A man in an FLR can gradually reorganise himself to do the majority of the housework, and can learn to cook, to clean and to do all these things to a high standard. He can go off to learn to cook and take classes. Many men in an FLR are able to take over the "domestic service" element of life at home.

In some households the woman is the main wage earner and the man is at home as a "househusband". In such cases it is important to get into a FLR situation to prevent him wasting time, doing things wrong, or just not delivering what She needs.

Money

There are so many rows in married life about money. How to get it and how to spend it and what needs to be saved for a rainy day. If the man and woman are in a FLR relationship money can form one of the areas where She takes over control. It may be just that She is better at managing it, or brings more of it into the relationship. Men often waste money on tools for DIY, magazines, drinks for friends and other things. If he hands over control of all his money matters to Her then this disappears. he is only given the money he needs and must account for all expenditure. The money does not get frittered away. Together the couple discuss how to pay the bills, the cheapest and most effective tariffs for utilities and where to get food with discounts. He then goes and does the buying and accounts to the woman. He is not permitted a credit card except for fuel and other essentials and it is scrutinized each month. In some household the pay packet is paid into a joint account and then transferred to the woman's account immediately on arrival.

This is no different from what was very common in many households in the past. The man was paid and went home to hand over his pay packet. That way there was money for food on the table and the bills to be paid, and he did not waste it on cigarettes and drink.

Control of money is an important part of an FLR. Here the man is showing the woman how much he trusts Her.

Free time

Many men waste their time reading magazines, surfing the net, (often for sex associated sites), and going out to drink with work colleagues after work. They go away for weekends for fishing or other pursuits to drink and play around. They sit in the armchair all weekend watching sport. In a FLR these are activities that the man agrees to have controlled by the Woman. She decides if he is to go out to drink with work colleagues otherwise he comes home. he will probably have chores to do anyway. She decides what websites he can use, and how long he can spend looking at sport on the TV or looking at action films. She controls the TV remote.

Many men who have been content to allow their partner to take over responsibility for sex and otherwise are doing their share and more of the housework still want to have "their own time". There is nothing wrong with this. But in an FLR there is discussion and agreement and then the woman decides. This frees up time for the couple to be together, keeps the man away from watching pornography and allow them both to do things together and to watch programs together.

Perhaps with this extra time the couple may want to exercise together or play a sport, learn a new skill, start a writing career, or just hang out together. This means they get closer together and so many of those rows caused by the man being off "enjoying himself" when he is needed at home disappear. One option here is to formalise the use of the TV remote control; She controls it, he agrees.

If holidays are agreed after open discussion with the woman having the final decision then there will not be trouble from a man booking a holiday for both which She does not want.

Direction of Development

Many couples just go on from day to day not thinking of the future. Many women have come out of the workplace to raise children and want to get back to it. Many men would like to learn new skills and develop themselves to be able to get better jobs. Older couples need to think about retirement, and every couple need to plan for the future.

This requires thinking, planning and open discussion and conflict arises when there is no discussion, there are unsaid assumptions, and both are not involved. In an FLR this can be another area in which the couple can agree how to go forward. The man and the woman will work together, but here as in the rest of FLR it may be the woman who makes the decisions.

Reality of FLR

There are thousands of couples living the FLR life without any part of the BDSM agenda, but there are others in whom it is a part of their DBSM life. Here the man is giving up power to his partner and Mistress and She is taking over control. He may describe himself as Her slave or property but the reality is that She will be making the decisions after discussion but with Her in control. There may be bondage, there may be punishment for failure to deliver on housework or other areas, but this is agreed as part of the slave contract and is not necessarily part of FLR.

For those who do not go down the BDSM path the opportunity is there for the man to show by his life that he is serving and caring for his partner. He realises areas in which She is better able to control things than him, e.g. money, and has willingly handed over control. The couple may have only started on the process of using FLR, and only use it for sex, or housework. They may have used the process successfully and now have all of the five "food groups" controlled by the woman.

So how might it look?

i have a complex life as i have a partner and She does not know of my desire to be a slave. i am also at the same time a slave and property to my Mistress.

At home we have not discussed domestic service or chastity or FLR but things have developed under the surface. When my partner had a major operation a few years ago i had to take over all housework and cooking. When She recovered i was able to express my desire to help out and do my share. Now it is assumed i will tidy up each night, do any washing up left over and leave the kitchen and living room clean and tidy. i will lay the breakfast and clear away my things and put them away when i get up first. In the evening i will prepare Her bed and turn it down. i will run Her bath when She wants me to, and occasionally, very rarely, give her a foot massage when She wants it. This is only when She wants it. i do some of the shopping and before i leave work for home each day i check with her whether there is anything She needs.

She has control of the remote control for the television, and decides where we go on holiday. She has control of sex, and knows that She can have what She wants and when She wants it. i am bound to chastity by my Mistress except when my wife requires sex. i am not allowed to initiate anything.

She has not got control over my money otherwise it would be difficult to find funds to provide things for Mistress and time with Mistress is time taken from work, for i have a relatively flexible work time. She has not yet taken control over our direction of development but i support anything She wants to do herself, and She has got me thinking, planning and talking about retirement.

So at home i am in sort of "stealth" FLR. But it is not really stealth because She knows that i am giving Her the control and although we have not discussed it, it is obvious that She likes being "spoiled" when i do the housework and the attention She gets. Now She controls sex totally She is much more relaxed about it and i get more, plus the chance to give oral sex as well when She wants it. No rows here as She is in control.

But i am also a slave to my Mistress who knows and supports all that is going on at home. To Her i am a slave so there is no sex only chastity and no masturbation. For Her there is work when She desires it and how She wants it. There is punishment if i get things wrong. And all the time i need to keep careful to make sure that nothing leaks to my home life. i did start kneeling to kiss my wife's feet and She seemed to like it, but Mistress has banned this and i am only to kiss Her feet. i gradually stopped doing it at home, and there was no comment, but i am sure if any of the tasks i regularly perform stopped there would be comment and sharp at that.

So FLR can occur in "vanilla relationships" but fits so well with the whole reality of being a slave that it is an important part of it as well. Of course here it is much more "Female Supremacy", power exchange, and the slave understanding his proper place.

(See also: chastity, domestic service, female supremacy, personal service, power exchange, training, submission)

F is for Fetish

The word fetish opens up a world of possibilities. It is used to describe types of clothing, certain lifestyles and at a deeper level it describes activity or ideas which cause arousal or in extreme cases can be the only way in which some people can be aroused or reach orgasm.

Fetish clothing may often be made of leather or latex, sometimes teamed up with high heels or boots. There may be bondage elements such as a collar or cuffs or chains as ornament and the appearance is out of the ordinary. Some people wear it for play at home, others at fetish parties where there is often a strict dress code and participants are expected to be dressed in fetish wear and not every day types of clothing. Some people like to go out in public dressed spectacularly in their fetish wear but this is uncommon.

Fetish lifestyles include the whole of dominance and submission, bondage and sadism and masochism (BDSM). This is the context in which i exist as a slave and my Mistress as a dominant. Those who describe themselves as Goths like to dress in their favourite black colour with heavy dark make up as part of their image. If i go out of doors with Mistress i might be expected to be wearing a steel collar, corset, chastity and chains and be on a lead but most of it is hidden under my outer clothing. The lead only appears out of the bottom of my jacket sleeve and nothing is obvious to those who see us in the street.

If Mistress wanted me to be out in public with the collar visible or dressed as a woman that is Her decision. My worry would be that people who know me in my outside life might see me and my BDSM life become common knowledge and known to my family. At gatherings of like minded individuals it is much easier for my collar to be visible. Even here there are often rules that genitals shall be covered up.

When fetish wear and activity is arousing there are many preferences. i love to see Mistress in Her latex or leather costumes or Her boots with Sharp heels but it is much more important to me that She is dressed as She wants to be. i find it equally arousing to see her long legs visible or her to have them covered up. Of course arousal gets me nowhere as i am locked away in a chastity device.

i find the whole fetish world of BSDM with bondage, beating, electrics, and the control my Mistress has over me and my submission extremely exciting. This is the fetish world that i like and enjoy. For me fetish wear, bondage apparatus and bondage, and serving Mistress both with domestic and personal service gives me such pleasure. i have also come to like the pain. Others get aroused by other things. Here are a few and a little about them. Adult baby: the person likes to be dressed in nappies and baby type clothes, wear a dummy and be treated as a baby.

Balloon: The person likes to have filled balloons pressed onto them and then burst.

Pony: The subject likes to be treated as a pony, harnessed and made to pull a cart, ridden by Mistress with a saddle or bare, controlled with a bridle, gag and reins and controlled just like a horse. They may be expected to sleep in a stable on straw and only to communicate with horse type noises and no speech.

Puppy: Here the subject is expected to stay in a puppy cage, to move around on all fours on a lead and to eat and drink with his face in a dog bowl. Food can be dog food or dog biscuits and he is treated more like a pet than a person.

Smoking; If Mistress sits smoking , just the act of her doing so excites some people. They may also desire to breathe in the smoke or to be an ashtray.

Scat: This applies to any activity involving faeces either with Mistress shitting over the slave or other activity including the slave licking her clean after She has been to the toilet.

Splodge: Splodge play is when there is use of food and other things to make everything messy. This includes the use of cream, soup, baked beans or spaghetti poured over the slave or rubbed into him. He becomes a total mess. If both Mistress and slave play this way both will be equally messy. Such play is often best done in a large play paddling pool to keep everything else clean and tidy.

Transvestitism: means a man dressing as a woman. This could be a man who likes dressing in woman's clothes and gets aroused by it but it also applies to a slave who is made to wear such apparel and made a sissy and forced into feminization. Here there is the activity but also the power issue as it is Mistress who decides what he shall wear with no escape from the humiliation.

These are only a few of those many activities described as fetishes. For me the arousal, the excitement and the pleasure all come from submission to Mistress
And the whole BDSM life including the fact that i have discovered myself to be a masochist as i now like to be flogged and beaten and shocked and enjoy the pain a long as it is not too severe. For others a single activity may be more important. This can include those who are into spanking and attend spanking parties even if they are not into the rest of BDSM or fetish wear.Everyone is a little bit different and how much fetish wear, activity or lifestyle they want depends on them. For me it depends on Mistress because my core fetish is being her slave and property.

(See also, Ashtray, boots, breath control, chastity, feet, forced feminization, fetish, hair, humiliation, latex, leather, military, medical, rubber, shopping, sissy, spanking, tights, trampling)

F is for Figging

If a lump of fresh ginger is peeled to remove its skin then pushed into the anus it starts to release chemicals that are irritant. This causes pain and makes it difficult to keep still.

As the ginger starts to warm up and break down and dissolve more of the chemicals are released and the slave is kept uncomfortable and irritated for several hours. It is important to make sure the ginger root has a stalk which is still outside so it can be pulled out if it becomes too unbearable.

This is a torment that Mistress has said She may use on me and i await it with trepidation. She has the pieces of ginger so I must wait my fate.

(See also: arse, heating cream, humiliation, ice)

F is for financial servitude

Some slaves seek to be in financial servitude to their Mistress. They know She needs to have money to fund Her lifestyle and that She is spending time and energy in controlling them. She has expenses which need to be filled. She is spending time controlling her slaves when She could be building her career and gaining financial reward, so unless She is independently wealthy She will need help.

Slaves can contribute to the expenses Mistress faces. She has household bills and so some slaves agree to sponsor a household bill, such as water, electricity or gas. Others may help to fund Her car. If a Mistress provides equipment to use on a slave, or purchases a chastity device or corset for her slave then it all costs money and he can and should provide it for Her.

So there are a lot of expenses and slaves can help to cover them. This can be through a standing order or direct debit to cover expenses, or providing funding for equipment, or even going on a shopping trip in attendance on Mistress and picking up the bills.

This is not payment for services. This is something else. It is a tribute provided voluntarily for the Mistress by her slave. She is a Mistress; not paid for service, but needing assistance with bills and with a slave who desires to assist and provides the "tribute" which shows he is serious in being a slave.

Of course if a slave sees something that Mistress would like, or identifies her favourite perfume, food or drink or clothing then they may wish to contribute for this as well.

Accepting a life of financial servitude to the electricity company on behalf of Mistress is just another way the slave shows he values Her.

When i attended Professional Mistresses in the past they charged by the time they spent with a client, just like any other therapist. Now i am slave and property it is my desire to provide tribute to the Mistress who owns me and deserves at least a tithe of my income. That is how it was in medieval times with villagers providing 10% or more of their produce for their Lord. That is how is with Mistress.

This is an integral part of my servitude to Her.

(See also: chastity, contracts, domestic service, shopping)

F is for Food Control

A Mistress can control the food a slave eats and how he does it. This can be a good way to control a slave's weight or get him into good eating habits. If every day the slave goes and sits in his car for his lunch of cat food and water She is controlling him. This is what Mistress does with me to prevent me eating too much or junk food and it works well. From time to time She changes the lunch from cat food to salad sandwiches, dog food, fish, or soup to define my lunchtime meal.

When i attend She may weigh me to check weight loss is continuing and i am not putting on weight but it is difficult to eat in a tight compression vest and pants so the stomach is compressed just like a corset so this reduces the amount i eat. Large meals bring pain and discomfort; small is good. Making me drink a litre of water with the cat food keeps me hydrated and the need to eat what Mistress has decided means i have to go to the car park and leave my desk. So She gets me to take a work break to eat as She wants.

But other times her control of my food intake is not so easy to take. i may be required to eat the hottest chillies or have my food laced with carpet fluff, earth, or cigarette ash. i eat what i am given and how Mistress wants it. She could add in edible grubs or insects and it would be my task to eat them. Of course sitting in my car eating my cat food i am able to use a spoon and i am sitting in comfort. Not so when i am with Mistress. Sometimes i am allowed the same food as Her on a plate sitting up at the table, but other times it is on a plate on the floor. From time to time without warning it is from a dog bowl with another of clean water nearby and i eat with my face in the bowl. No hands to help to prevent it being smeared all over my face.

Sometimes i have been fed blindfolded so that i have no idea of what I have
coming next to swallow either nice or nasty. It all shows Mistress controls my food.

Food control by Mistress means the amount, type and nature of the food is defined by Mistress. It shows Her control over all parts of me. If She wants me to eat like an animal it is because as a slave i am an animal if Mistress decides it.

When we are out together Mistress allows me to eat with Her . Nice but She does have the electric controller including a wire to my butt plug electrics so even where it all looks so normal i can be disturbed with severe shocks. Allowed to eat but each mouthful might mean a shock. Food control really allows Mistress the opportunity to use Her wicked sense of humour to full effect and gives me the opportunity to submit.

(See also: contracts, electrics, exercise, training)

F is for Feet and Foot worship

i am so lucky to have a Mistress with the most beautiful feet. It is lovely to see them, fabulous to kneel to kiss them and wonderful to be required to give Her a foot massage from time to time.

Mistress knows where She wants massaging and how hard. She knows what She wants done with her feet and how far up the leg i may go.

On arrival in her presence i am always to kneel at Her feet and prostrate myself before Her and then i can see Her feet and nothing else. i am allowed to kiss Her feet when She allows it but must never kiss the feet of anyone else ever.

i can be used as a footstool to lift Her feet and rest them when She is tired. She can use her feet to kick me and prod me especially when She wants me at Her feet. i am required to kneel at Her feet in public on attending Her no matter how public the place may be; an airport, a restaurant, a train station, at the shops or just out in the street.

For some slaves the Mistress's feet are such an object of beauty that they worship them. Only seeing her feet or thinking of them can they get any erection; of course this assumes they can get one anyway and are not locked away in a chastity device to prevent such activity.

Mistress has the feet that matter to me as a slave, but i have to keep my feet in good condition for Mistress. Mistress expects that the feet of her slaves should always be clean, non smelly and have well cropped nails. She expects slaves to remove hard and dry skin and to make sure all the skin is acceptable. i have had to get cream to remove hard skin and use sandpaper on the feet to make the skin smooth and Mistress has warned me that i will be taken and be given a pedicure. She has also indicated that if my feet are not acceptable then i will be given a severe beating.

Mistress has the feet which deserve care and worship but they can also be used to crush a slave, to trample upon him, and to be placed on his neck to force him to the floor and remind him that he is a slave and no more than a worm to be crushed under Her heel.

Sometimes i am allowed to see Mistress's feet but other times She wears high heels, shoes or boots so they are hidden. But even then adorned in all Their glory they are a sign of Her power over all parts of Her slave. Her feet are fabulous and beautiful; my feet are not but are there to serve.

(See also: Boots, kicking, personal service, training, trampling,)

F is for Forced Feminization

Some slaves want to dress as a woman and like to wear female clothes. Some Mistresses want their slaves to act as domestic servants in livery or dressed as a "French maid". Other slaves actively want to lose their male characteristics and to look and act as a woman and Mistress may wish to help them in this and to guide them away from their masculinity.

Mistress can order their slaves to remove body hair or to wax their private parts and to have them pulled back underneath them so that they are not apparent. They can be reminded to wear their chastity device 24/7 so they are fully locked away.

But some slaves want to be forced to be feminized, including even the use of hormones to grow breasts, plucking of eyebrows and wearing female attire all the time. This can be required by the Mistress. Forced feminization is not really a true description of this process as it has been agreed and consented to by the male slave. The picture of forced feminization where the slave is truly forced into this state by a Mistress is a fantasy most common in books and on line but not in reality where consent is needed.

Mistress can make her slaves wear female pants, tights and corsets under their clothing with corselets and even bras. This is to control them, to crush them with the tight clothing, and to humiliate them and emasculate them and to show them that no part of them is free from Mistress's control.

For me forced feminization has not formed part of my life as a slave to my Mistress. When i do domestic service She has me dressed in "Her" livery with trousers, tea shirt and jacket. i do not desire to be dressed in women's clothes or to lose my manhood.

But i am happy to have it constrained by the steel chastity that i wear and by the orders from Mistress that ban me utterly from masturbation.

Despite this i am sitting here typing this section in very tight support tights, an elastane corselet and vest under my clothes. i do not feel this is forced feminization, but the wish of my Mistress to control and crush me. i have been informed that a corset comes next to crush me even further. Even though i am waxed to remove all hairs from my penis, balls, crack and nipples i still feel the same. This is what Mistress wishes for Her male slave and i am here to submit and obey.
This is not forced feminization but there are many slaves who would like to try it and many also who have experienced it and enjoyed every minute and day.

(See also contracts, compression clothing and corsets, humiliation, ownership, sissy, training)

F is for Furniture

Mistress spends much of her time on her feet and needs to put her feet up when She has the opportunity. So She needs a footstool. This is a good opportunity for a slave to serve. He can crouch on all fours to provide a footstool or lie at her feet. Either way he may need to stay in position for a long time particularly if Mistress is watching Her favourite television program. A kneeling slave on all fours can also act as a seat when Mistress wants something to sit upon. Again he must learn to stay totally still under his Mistress's weight. Some Mistresses make it easier for the slave by attaching him to a bondage frame or using bondage to keep him in position in the position She has decided. Either way he will stay where he has been placed.

At a party Mistress may need somewhere to hang coats and a slave can function as a hat stand or candle holder to hold lighted candles for illumination. She may want to put ashtrays around the room for guests who smoke and a slave can kneel with an open mouth to function as an ashtray

One thing is clear. The slave is no longer a person but he is just a piece of furniture to be used. He can be covered with a rug or sheet to keep him out of sight or left naked in position. Mistress can put him on the floor on his back with knees raised and use him to support a table top for Her to use to eat Her supper or have a dinner party. He can be kept in position for hours and needs to learn to keep still. Furniture does not have a voice so he must be silent even when Mistress pokes him with a sharp stiletto heel. Some Mistresses demand silence from their slaves when they turn them into furniture; others use a gag. Whatever the method this is a good way to turn a slave into no more than an object to be used by Mistress.

my experience is mainly being a footstool though Mistress occasionally uses me as a seat. i have been turned into the base of a table but it was difficult to arrange things to keep the surface totally flat and level. For me it was yet another way to be allowed to serve Mistress so She can be comfortable and relax.

Specialised furniture can be a part of any dungeon or play room and it is possible to purchase flat pack dungeon furniture which can be put away when not in use. Cages, racks, whipping benches, or other furniture to which a slave can be attached can all be obtained without great difficulty. Alternatively the slave can be shown pictures from catalogues and be required to build the items himself. Normal household furniture can be customised to allow for bondage points to be fitted, whether a chair, a table or a bed. Wardrobes and cupboards can be used to confine a slave. Anything will do. A second hand chair can be modified to make a throne for Mistress or a bondage chair for the slave, with or without the seat. The possibilities are endless.

(See also: ashtray, bondage, cage, cupboard, humiliation, rack, stocks, training, X position for whipping, whipping bench,)

F is for Flogging

i do not have any favourite flogger, but i do like being flogged by Mistress.

She enjoys herself when She flogs and beats me and i enjoy that partly because She is enjoying herself, and partly because it does feel good, even when it hurts a lot.

Beating, caning, paddling, spanking and flogging can all be seen as punishment, and have been used like that on me in the past. After i broke out of chastity and masturbated the sentence from Mistress was harsh. There was a sentence of 1000 strokes. The strokes were given over several visits, but the power of the strokes was hard, and each time my backside was left swollen and a little bruised, and my back felt sore afterwards. That was definite punishment for a serious misdemeanour, but most often flogging is just part of my life and the times i am allowed to attend Her.

It just feels good to be prepared for a beating, hooded in the heavy leather hood, strapped up tight so all i can do is breathe, or blindfolded and gagged to keep me quieter during the beating. Mistress is kind and allows me to use an inflatable butterfly gag, and although my arms are cuffed i can inflate and deflate the gag myself. This means that it does not make me gag but allows me to inflate it hard when the blows are coming fast and painfully so i can keep silent as Mistress wishes.

She always takes time warming me up, usually with blows from her hand, and a brisk spanking. The backside feels as red as it probably is. Then She chooses from her range of favourites. All the time She is changing Her point of aim to cover the whole of my behind and the upper thighs. Sometimes She gets bored with this and starts on the soles of my feet. Some of the strokes are soft, no more than a soft caress, but the next one might be given with the full force of Her arm and i have no idea what is coming next.

Once warmed up She changes to the floggers, one which is soft, but heavy and lands with a loud and hard thud, sometimes so hard as to push the wind out of my chest, and the other which has smaller strands and bites. She alternates these, striking across the whole of the upper back, my thighs and the already smarting backside. She also has one which is rubber and although soft to touch can be very painful and one made of chain links with many thin chains which stings and She can also use it to flog my nipples.

If the pain becomes too great i am allowed to beg for "mercy" This means that She stops hitting that part and changes implement and site of target. Not an end but just some other way to beat me. i know that i can trust Mistress and that She will hurt me with the beating, but never allow me to come to harm, or be permanently marked.

If i was in extremis She would know, and i know She would stop if i really asked her to do so. So it is all safe and consensual and i love it.

Mistress does so enjoy beating me, and occasionally gets carried away with enthusiasm. i can tell from the increasing frequency and the pattern of the strokes that She is really engaged, and it is so good to have an opportunity for giving her this fun.

Sometimes the beating goes on for over an hour, and at the end i am left still trussed up, bent over the stool or the whipping bench, still in the dark as She walks away. i have no idea of when She is coming back, and whether the beating will resume. She could have just gone off for a cup of tea or to use the toilet.

By this stage i am lost in a haze of pain and pleasure, stinging from all the blows, with a backside that feels so swollen, and indeed when i am eventually released it often looks just like that, swollen and red, but rarely left with marks. i am finally allowed to kneel up and the hood is removed, and i find myself in the light again with Mistress there in front of me. i feel totally wrung out, pleasured, and fulfilled and i have had another good flogging from Mistress.

It is not always like that, for often the beating will be stopped so Mistress can have a time working on my nipples, twisting them, pulling them, using Her cruel sharp nails, or striking them and the front of my chest with a small whip as well.

Mistress occasionally decides to sit down upon me with all Her weight to hold me still, and then with my backside before Her the target is so close and available.

On a few occasions i have been due to fly abroad and Mistress will use the cane to beat and mark me, so i fly with a criss-cross of cane marks on my backside. This means the sitting for hours in the plane is more difficult, and i find myself squirming in my seat to get comfortable. This does have the effect of keeping me moving and is Mistress's idea to prevent clots forming in the legs on long haul flights.

Being flogged and beaten by Mistress is so exciting, so arousing, and so much fun. The pain is severe but never more than i can take, and She has trained me to be able to take more over several years. Now i look forward to a flogging when i see Mistress, and feel i have missed out if it is not possible.

She enjoys herself. i enjoy myself. Both of us are having fun. i treasure the floggings Mistress gives me, and at the time get so into it that all i want sometimes is more, and more, and more. Luckily there are times when i am able to spend 24 hours or longer, or occasionally a whole week with Mistress and then there is at least one daily flogging, and often more. It is now just a part of my submission, my slavery, and Her power over my body which She owns. It is Her totally owned buttocks and back She is scourging, they just happen to be attached to my body and are there for Her pleasure. No favourite flogger, but flogging by Mistress is so wonderful.

(See also arse, cane, crop, discipline, paddle, punishment, spanking, tawse, whip,)

G is for Gags and gagging a slave

Slaves may be required to keep silent for their Mistress. If She is doing things that may make them make a noise She may want them silenced with a gag, or She may want to listen to their screams and cries as she torments them. It is Her decision.

Gags stop a slave using their mouth to talk. They can be made simply by using wide rolls of sticky tape wound round and round the head, allowing the slave to breathe through their nose but nothing from the mouth. There is often a strap around the head or a head harness with a ball or cylinder to force between the teeth and keep the mouth open. One problem with this sort of gag is that it fills up the front of the mouth, and if this happens or if the slave vomits then the vomit cannot get out and there is a risk of it going down into the lungs with dire results.

Sometimes gags incorporate a part which sticks into the mouth, like a dildo or plug to go right to the back of the mouth. This fills up the whole mouth and can cause the slave to want to be sick as it touches the back of the throat. Often in BDSM fiction a slave is gagged by having their mouth filled with pants pushed inside and then taped in place. This also fills the mouth and can lead to the slave wanting to be sick. Some slaves can handle this sort of gagging but others cannot take it.

One option is to use a rubber butterfly gag with a latex bladder inside the front of the mouth which can be inflated to fill up and become larger filling the front part of the mouth and with a hard rubber pad on the outside of the mouth to keep the bag inside. i find this a good way to be gagged as Mistress allows me to control the amount of air in the gag. If the pain from the whipping or caning is getting severe i inflate the gag to the maximum to stop me making any noise, and if I begin to feel that i might be sick i deflate the bag so it sits just behind the teeth. This is very good of Mistress who could of course just blow up the gag and leave me tied down helpless and at Her mercy unable to speak or make a noise.

One form of gag which is good for those who find gags make them feel sick is a ring gag where a rubber or steel ring is placed in the mouth, and the mouth is held open. The slave then has an open mouth which he cannot close, and other things can then be put in there including plugs, cigarette ash or anything else the Mistress decides including a strap on dildo.

Dentists and Surgeons use a medical gag which fits around the teeth and which is used to hold the mouth open for surgical procedures where the mouth must remain open. The Whitehead gag is one variety of this sort of gag and can also be purchased from BDSM suppliers and it is good for use on slaves.

If a Mistress truly wants to stop up the mouth of a slave, and the slave is prepared for the risks of only being able to breathe through his nose and the risk of not being able to open his mouth at all then superglue can be applied to the lips to seal the mouth. A slave whose mouth has been closed with superglue is mute and can make no sound at all. Mistress needs to keep the superglue remover solution ready available in case there are problems and She needs to dissolve the glue rapidly. One problem of this sort of "muting " of a slave is that when the glue is removed it can remove some of the skin of the lips as well and leave ulcerated lips which take time to heal and look like severe cold sores. Wax can also be tried but it is not as effective.

My experience with gags is that i find difficulty with anything inside my mouth which reaches towards the palate and the back of the mouth. Touching those areas makes me want to heave and be sick and has made dental treatment difficult in the past. i can cope with a ball gag which is part split to go part in front of my teeth and part behind, a surgical gag, or the inflatable latex butterfly gag which i have described above. Mistress has made me mute on a couple of occasions in the past with superglue. Both occasions lead to the production of small sores on the lips but that could be because i tried to open my mouth before all the glue had dissolved. On the first occasion i was kept muted for several hours including a long drive with me sitting in the front of the car. This was very successful. On a second occasion i had been given tasks to perform and exercising muted it was difficult to breathe as my nose became partially blocked

These experiences plus all that is written on the subject of gagging a slave makes me agree entirely with the idea that no slave should be left on his own after being gagged.
Mistress needs to stay with the slave who is gagged so that if there is any distress, vomiting or choking She can remove the gag immediately. But most times a Mistress wants to gag he slave it is so She can do things to him and She will be there with him all the time.

Gagging a slave allows the Mistress yet another area of his life where She is in total control. It silences noisy slaves who talk too much and prevents neighbours and those outside hearing the moans of a slave who is being tormented by his Mistress. It is also very humiliating for a slave to be there gagged, drooling with saliva running out of his mouth and with no way to shut his mouth at all. Of course if a slave has a tongue piercing a simple gag is a cord from the tongue out of the mouth to stop him moving his tongue. Similarly a nipple clamp attached to the tongue is both painful and makes it very difficult for a slave to talk at all.

(See also: ashtray, bondage, clamps, dildo, humiliation, medical, quiet with slave kept in silence, training)

H is for Hair

Control of the hair on a slave is a good way for a Mistress to show Her power over him. She can decide on the style of his haircut, and how far his eyebrows are trimmed. She decides when he goes to the barber and how much comes off. She wants He slave to look as She wants him to be.

She can control his outwards appearance and even more the hair that is not seen in public. If She wants him to have all his body hair shaved off or removed with wax strips this is Her decision. If She wants him to shave his penis, balls, and pubic hair, or to have all the hair removed from these areas and the crack through to the buttocks as well, then She sends him off to have a Brazilian or Hollywood wax treatment.

She decides if he is to be allowed facial hair, sideboards, or a moustache or beard. She could decide that She wants all his hair removed and his head shaved bare all the time. So She shows Her control over the slave by all She does and how She deals with his hair. In my case my partner and Mistress both want me clean shaven on the face so that is OK. My partner decides when i am sent to the barber and how much is removed, whether my eyebrows are trimmed and anything else. She makes the appointments and just informs me when i am to attend. She talks to the hairdresser and they discuss what She wants done. No option for me at all.

My Mistress has ideas of how She wants my body hair. She initially had me shaving my penis and balls and around my nipples. Now i am sent for waxing by a professional therapist who knows i am a slave. It would be a little difficult to hide it when i am wearing my collar and ankle and wrist chains for an appointment. After the first visit i was inspected by Mistress who said She was satisfied with the work. i had already had to book my next appointment and this is now the way it will be. i am on a regular waxing schedule so i look as Mistress wants me to be. She has control and it is my pleasure to submit to the changes She wants on my body. She also controls my food intake and diet, and wants me to lose weight. All of these are examples of Her working to develop Her slave and property.

But Mistresses have hair also. They know how they want to look, how they want their hair shampooed, and how they like their hair brushed to remove tangles. Mistress has lovely hair, and keeps it so well. It frames Her beautiful face and looks good, lustrous, and wavy.

Some Mistresses like their slaves to brush their hair, and this is wonderful for a slave, to be allowed to touch Mistress's hair and to smell it and brush it smooth. A few have had their slaves trained to wash and shampoo, and fix their hair for them, but this requires training and must always be done right.

(See also: Brazilian wax, exercise, food control, personal care, training, wax)

H is for handcuffs

The police and other law enforcement agencies put handcuffs on those they arrest to control them. The cuffs go around each wrist and they are linked together so that the wrists can be secured either in front of behind the subject. In the USA handcuffs are often combine with leg cuffs and a waist chain to make it difficult for prisoners to escape custody.

Handcuffs can be easily carried in a purse or a bag by Mistress and applied to her slave when She wants to use them quickly and effectively. They are locked and She has the key. The slave is helpless. The slave now has hard steel bands around his wrists and may be able to do little with his hands. He is at the mercy of his Mistress. Handcuffs are very good for quickly securing a slave but difficult to wear for long periods as the steel rubs and chafes and marks the wrists. Other cuffs made of leather or rubber can be used instead, wrapped around the wrists and each one locked into place. Then they can be linked with locks or chain and the slave is controlled. But these can be worn for hours or even days.

Most Mistresses have at least a couple of pairs of handcuffs but may also have leg cuffs or leg irons for the ankles and thumb cuffs with a very small cuff which fits around a thumb or big toe.

In the past much heavier steel cuffs were used around wrist and ankles which are often termed manacles. They can also be combined in a steel framework to join neck, wrists, and ankles together which keeps the slave unable to straighten up. This has been called "the "jailers daughter" and is an instrument of torture for a slave left in this will start to suffer from severe cramps as he cannot stretch and he is left in them for hours at a time

Mistress has thumb cuffs, handcuffs, leg irons, manacles and locking leather cuffs to imprison me. They allow Her to control me and to keep me secure in bondage and I never know which of them She will use. They work well so that when i see Her bring them out I know i am in for secure inescapable bondage. If the wrists are secured with cuffs and a coat is put on top so hide them the slave can be transported out in public. Cuffs can also be secured with chain and locks to a car seat or a place in the car boot so that the slave is locked away easily.

(See also: bondage, chains, cuffs, manacles)

H is for heating cream

Heating creams containing capsaicin or oil of wintergreen are rubbed into the skin to warm it up and help with stiff or painful muscles and relieves pain. But the chemicals involved are irritant to the nerve endings in the skin and can give a feeling of heat and burning.

If the heating cream is rubbed into the cock or balls or around the anus or nipples or on a backside already tender form beating the slave feels the whole area is on fire. It is just like being rubbed with nettles which cause pain, swelling and reddening to the skin.

Mistress can apply enough cream to me to make things on fire for hours, and if it is applied to the inside of a pair of pants the slave can be kept in agony for hours or all day.

The creams are easy to obtain from any supermarket or Chemists. A small amount goes a long way and the burning lasts for hours. Even removal of the cream does not cool things down. It is an easy and simple and cheap way to torment a helpless slave.

(See also figging, ice, wax)

H is for hoods

A slave who is blindfolded cannot see and becomes more vulnerable but the blindfold may slip and let in the light. So using a hood to keep a slave in the dark may be better and more effective. The hood may be made of rubber and be tight, with mouth and nose holes, so the slave can breathe but no holes for the eyes so he cannot see. Fabric can be used to cover the head, even a canvas bag, but the slave needs to be able to breathe and a bag over the head may make breathing difficult. Elasticated fabric provides a thin breathable bag to grip the head tightly but still allow the slave easy breathing. There is little light coming through the bag, but in combination with a blindfold there is no light at all. It can all be combined with a blindfold or even putting the salve in totally black opaque contact lenses.

This makes the slave vulnerable; every sense is activated and anything done to him is more intense. He has a degree of sensory deprivation and cannot see what is coming next. But there are also heavier hoods made of leather with lacing up the back or a zip, and straps to pull the hood tight around the head. There are inflatable rubber ones made of latex. The slave is zipped into the hood and the breathing hole positioned then the hood is blown up tight. Both of these types of hoods give a much more intense experience as the whole head is being crushed. They are not for those who are claustrophobic but they are wonderful to wear.

Once a slave is put in the hood his features are gone, and he is unidentifiable which is why a hood may be good if he is to be paraded around at a party where he might not want to be spotted. Hooded he has also lost his identify and is just a slave in a hood so it helps remove any personality and emphasise his state. If the hood is inflated or is a heavy leather hood then it is easy for the

Mistress to slap and punch the hood knowing that the slave will feel it but he is protected by the hood material.

i am lucky that my Mistress has a range of hoods, inflatable rubber, heavy leather, rubber, and fabric which She can use. i lose all idea of time and become disorientated in a hood, and the lighter ones can also be used for all night sessions or even longer. Being a hooded slave emphasises the total power Mistress has over me and it is so, so good when the hood is removed and I am allowed to see Her face again.

(See also, blindfolds, darkness and disorientation, leather, latex, overnight sessions, pressure)

H. is for Humiliation

Many slaves like to be humiliated by their Mistress either in private or even in public. They like Her to use her power to "take them down a notch" and to show them that they are no more than a worm.

This can be carried out in a wide variety of ways but all emphasise the worthlessness of the slave. It can be the way the slave is addressed by his Mistress, the tone She uses or the words She uses to him or about him. She can point out to him again and again that he is worthless and has no value. It can be the way She treats him with distain as no more than a slug.

He can be humiliated by having his manhood caged and being put in chastity so he is no longer a full man but one whose penis is controlled. That can be associated with the Mistress also pointing out to him how small he is in this area. She can make him wear women's pants or tights or a bra so that he knows he is Hers and no longer free, but if he were found out to be wearing such stuff it would be so humiliating. She can require him to be shaved or waxed. It is potentially humiliating for a man to be sent to have all the hair on his private parts removed and to have to say to the therapist why this is happening.

She can do so many things to humiliate Her slave but it is all in context. i have been put on a regular Brazilian waxing regime and the therapist knows i am a slave but i do not find it humiliating rather liberating because here is somewhere i can proclaim that i am a slave to the most wonderful Mistress. i am made to wear tight tights and a corselet and an elastane vest but i do not feel humiliated. i feel crushed as it is designed to do but i feel i am wearing these things because Mistress wants it and my desire is to submit to Her and to obey Her. If She were to dress me as a woman it is not something i desire and i would find it very difficult, but i would obey her because that is what a slave does and it is my delight to submit and obey.

So for some one thing is humiliating and of others it is not. Verbal humiliation has never been a way with my Mistress; She is more likely to praise me for having a body which She has developed. To her should go the praise not me. But there are slaves who get aroused and excited when they are verbally abused, sworn at, and it is pointed out that they have a small penis and balls almost too small to find. They enjoy being humiliated by Mistress either in public or private. i find whatever Mistress does with me an opportunity to submit and obey so i do not feel humiliated more free as her slave

(See also: ashtray, Brazilian wax, chastity, domestic service, domination, enema, forced feminization, ownership, power exchange, shopping, sissy, training)

H is for humbler

A humbler is a device which fits around the balls and is attached from the back to pull the balls back between the thighs. It consists of two curved pieces of wood with cut outs for the balls which fit closely between the thighs and are curved to stay in place. The balls are pulled back and placed between the plates and the two plates are screwed together. Now the slave has his balls pulled back and has to stay on his hands and knees.

If the knees are kept bent it is reasonably comfortable but if the slave attempts to stand or to straighten the legs then the balls are pulled backwards and the pain becomes intense. This keeps the slave on his knees where he belongs. If he is placed in the humbler and is lying down then he cannot straighten his legs so if left like that overnight then any attempt to stretch brings immediate pain. He cannot lie on his face or his back with the legs out.

These two simple plates of wood enable the Mistress to keep her slave on his knees where he belongs. It teaches him to be more humble and not to expect to be able to stand up. He lives on his knees and is fixed in this position. he must be humble for if he is not then the pain is intense and he may be kept in the device longer.

Some humblers have electrical contacts built in with one contact on each plate. This allows the Mistress to shock the slave whilst he is in the humbler giving Her even more power over him.

Mistress has just obtained a new humbler to use on me. i have worn one for her in the past that we made with two bamboo canes and rubber bands to hold them together. This was very tight and tended to make my balls turn purple in colour but it was very effective. The new one is more comfortable and can be worn for longer periods but both are totally effective in keeping me in my place. my place is on my knees, humble before Mistress.

(See also bondage, CBT, cuffs, chains, rope, training)

I is for Isolation

Isolating a slave is a good way to show that Mistress is in control. The slave is put away out of the way and left. He may be hooded or in chains. He is put out of the way in a cupboard or cage, or secured in a body bag. Mistress has left him. He cannot see and may have had his ears plugged up as well, or be subject to random noises or music to disorientate him.

For many years i have known that i find it "relaxing" in some strange way to be put in bondage, helpless, and isolated with the aid of a hood or blindfold. i find that my mind is always full of thoughts, mainly from work and other stresses, and they chase each other around and around and keep me awake at night. At home i am often still thinking of the day and its work when i should be concentrating on other things. Even in sessions with Mistress the outside world intrudes and spoils things. So a period of isolation and "down "time is often necessary to get me in the "zone" for serious fun and enjoyment.

This was particularly the first time i ever was able to be away from home for a whole night of bondage many years ago. i had driven far, and was so wound up that i could not relax so what should have been a wonderful time was marred by thoughts of work and other things.

Mistress has found that there are times when at least a couple of hours of a session may be needed with me in isolation, and there have been times when i have needed much more. Mistress says

"When I first met you one of the biggest needs for you was to calm down with hood in isolation for as long as it took you to calm down, sometimes 1 hour, other times 24 hrs. This was imperative you had this isolation to leave your worries and enter a calm state and then I could build you up to be in the ZONE. The psychological effects were immense. Other times being hooded and flogged right away was an immediate release for you."

She is so right. When i arrive to attend Mistress i go down on my knees and prostrate myself before Her. She knows me so well that She can gauge my state, and she always knows the stresses i am under at work and at home as well. She takes me, hoods me, and places me either in the cupboard which is locked to keep me in the dark, or in some other form of isolation and leaves me. On occasions She has had things to do so has left me alone in the house.

i sit there, or lie there, either enclosed or naked apart from my bonds. i am helpless and unable to move around. My head is covered by a hood, or at the very least i am blindfolded. i enter a strange world where i know i cannot do anything, and i must wait. This allows me to start to unwind, and over the hour or hours the tensions leave me, and i start to "stop". The thoughts which run round and round in my mind gradually are replaced by a blank space. i can think of Mistress; i can wonder what is to come next, but i cannot think.

This puts me into a frame of "living in the moment" and is such a rarity in the rest of my life. If the time is prolonged then i sometimes begin to get a little spooked by the silence. i really know i am safe, but i begin to worry that the whole afternoon has gone by and i am going to be late to leave and get home. Then i use Mistress's mantra to calm me down and all returns to normal.

By the time i am released from the silence and the isolation i am calm, and ready for whatever Mistress wishes to do. i am there for Her and time has no meaning. Indeed i often have no idea how long I have been kept in the isolation.

Occasionally i am able to get away for a night, or a few nights, as being "away on business or at a meeting" and then the isolation can be used to a much fuller extent. If i am really away at a meeting and away from both home and Mistress then Mistress requires me to sleep in a hood and chains, sometimes on the floor wrapped in a rubber sheet. This puts me into isolation until the alarm goes in the morning. i wake in chains and darkness and it takes me time to realise where i am and what i am doing. This is self imposed isolation, but on the orders of Mistress.

If i am away from home but with Mistress She controls my isolation. There is a time when She decides it is time for me to be put down for the night. She secures me. She hoods me. She checks that all will be safe. She is always so careful to make sure i will be safe and cannot get into any difficulty. This does not mean that i will necessarily be comfortable. i may be in a bag, or wrapped in a rubber sheet, and will be in restraints so i cannot touch myself as well. We have a straight jacket which is very effective to keep me under control. But the greatest control is over my sight, as i am hooded or blindfolded, and so i stay for the rest of the night, until Mistress wishes me to be moved.

The evening before may have been intense, with bondage, flogging, hot wax, or whatever Mistress has decided, but the isolation puts me asleep in minutes. No worries, no thoughts of work, just silence and oblivion. Of course during the night i wake often in pain or discomfort from my position and inability to move, sometimes with cramps from keeping in the same position. i may awake with the feeling of my cock being crushed as the steel chastity does its work. i may be in nipple clamps so the nipples feel they are so swollen, and i am often required to wear a butt plug as well.

It is not these things that have the effect on me but the silence, the isolation that Mistress has used on me. i wake in bondage and to the pleasure of knowing that i am secured, and i am controlled and that Mistress is in control. The night may be long, but it is always so good. Eventually, when convenient to Her, Mistress releases me, and i am allowed to see the light and Her face. But it might not be so. She might have decided to keep me hooded and in the dark for the rest of the day.

When it is possible to be with Mistress for days at a time then isolation at night and whenever She sees it necessary during the day always pays dividends. It makes what comes next, whether a flogging, more bondage, or being allowed to see Her face and serve Her in any way even more special. To spend every night for a week in a hood at Her orders is better than a month of holiday for its effects on me. On occasions we have travelled together to stay in dungeon chambers that can be hired by the night or day. then i am often transported in chains and hood in the back of the car. i have no idea of where i am going, or how long i stay there. Mistress may leave me and go shopping on the way. It is completely safe as there is always air and Mistress makes sure i do not get too hot or cold, but it is total isolation and it works its magic so i am ready, prepared, and eager for anything that comes after.

For me isolation is a powerful way in which Mistress prepares me for things She is going to do to me. She uses it to allow me to relax, and to get into a zone where i am ready to serve, and other things are blotted out. i can live in the moment. i can use all my energy to serve. i can be Hers totally. She controls it. She decides its duration. She decides what is done to me when in isolation. It is one of the most powerful things She does to me, and i do enjoy it so much, both at the time and in anticipation, and in thinking about it afterwards.

(See also; blindfold, bondage, bondage bags, cage, cupboard, hood, overnight sessions, training)

I is for Ice

Heat and cold can be used to stimulate a slave and applied to those tender and sensitized parts where it will have the most effect. To a slave who is hooded and in the dark both cold and heat often feel almost the same, though there is a world of difference between hot molten wax being dripped on the nipples and the touch of a block of ice. Both stimulate the same nerves and give slightly different but overlapping sensations which are different from hitting, pinching and striking the skin.

Mistress has used ice cubes to torment me often applying them when i least expect them to the nipples. But She has also used ice in other ways. On one occasion i was made to get into a bath of ice and water which was so painful. By the time i had been in the ice for a few minutes i was shaking uncontrollably and shivering. On another occasion She has had me on all fours and pushed ice cubes inside my back passage.

One particular trick is to make me dip my penis and balls into a bowl of liquid paraffin wax which will coat it and solidify and then to do the same into a bowl of ice. i am made to stay in the wax or the ice for equivalent periods. After a few cycles of this the parts are coated with hard wax and the feeling of heat and cold gets less but it is very intense to begin with, only getting less as the thickening layer of wax insulates the parts imprisoned underneath.

Ice is just one of the ways in which Mistress applies heat and cold to me. i could be placed outside on a cold day or in a room with no heating and i will rapidly become cold and start to shiver. Alternatively the room can be kept hot and i can be placed in a rubber bag so i am heated up and cooked in my own juices. i find that either being made very cold or very hot has the effect of making it more difficult for me to cope with anything else that is being done to me. Flogging feels more fierce. Bondage feels more severe, and i have difficulty staying focussed. But anyone with a fridge has ice cubes they can use on their slaves, and bags of ice are easy to obtain from the supermarket.

(See also: blindfold, heating cream, hood, isolation, nipples, rubber, wax)

J is for Judgement

Mistress holds so much power over me. i am her slave and She has the power to control me and to punish me if i fail her in any way. She inspects me; She inspects any work that i do for Her. If there is a failure She sits in majesty and passes judgement upon me.

Sometimes the punishment is swift and at other times it is spread out over several weeks. But it always happens as She has decided. There is no appeal. She is a kind Mistress but who requires obedience from Her slaves. Failure is punished as She decides. For all crimes the risk is of being dismissed from Her presence, and no slave wants that. So attendance on Mistress when She sits in judgement on you as a slave is always a worrying time.

The first time i found myself on my knees in front of Mistress in her judicial capacity i was really worried. i had been ordered to a state of chastity, but only wearing my device 15 hours per day, as it is not possible at night. But i was required to desist from masturbation 24/7. One night in the bath i started to touch myself and it happened. Immediate fear of what Mistress might say, coupled with a feeling that i must not try to hide my crime but must inform Her.

So i let Her know that i had failed her and waited. i waited and waited for her response. The response came when She wanted it to and She let me stew as i waited. i was condemned and She sat there in all her power and pronounced the verdict. i was fined a lot of money. That was the easy part. i was condemned to a hard beating of hundreds of strokes, spread out over time. That was difficult. i was condemned to 6 months in total chastity except when my partner wanted sex. No masturbation. No initiation of sex except on Mistress's orders. That was going to be much harder.

In the British criminal law a sentence once served is past. It remains on the records, and can be taken into consideration if the criminal commits further crimes but otherwise he is free. This is not the situation with Mistress. Her system of justice allows her to revisit sentences even up until the last moment of a sentence, and the felon can be hauled back to the court for a sentence to be prolonged. No freedom after this type of sentence but the uncertainty of what may follow.

i have already been returned to the court twice, and my sentence of chastity has been prolonged. Initially it was for 6 months, with initiation of sex with my partner dependant upon Mistress. Then it was prolonged for a further 9 months with no initiation allowed, and then a further period. So from the initial sentence it has been 18 months so far and with more to come.

Once convicted i can be returned to the court at any time; Mistress has decided that it is time to review my sentence again. There have been no further failings with masturbation but other crimes will be taken into consideration. i have been required to provide the court papers for Mistress to consider. With this system of law there is no defence and no defence is possible for i am a felon convicted by Her. There is only Her mercy. So now i wait again for the sentence of the court.

She decides and uses the format given in the judgement paper below.

This all has the effect of allowing me as a slave to kneel before my Mistress when She sits in judgement upon me whilst She is able to use her power to decide my fate and my punishment. It is a quasi-judicial process, similar but different to that used in courts of law to emphasise the power and majesty of Mistress.

Many other Mistresses use similar systems, and many slaves have a weekly assessment meeting with their Mistress when decisions are taken as to their failings during the week and they are given the appropriate punishment. This can be added to any regular beating that is already scheduled for that night anyway.

Punishments are entirely at the whim and decision of the Mistress. If a slave likes to be flogged or beaten then the beating can be made so intense that it is not something he will like, otherwise confinement, or any other thing that Mistress knows he will not like can be used. If She wishes he can be informed that he will be punished in this way but not allowed to know what will happen. he may have a date but no idea of the horror that awaits him.

(See also: chastity, contracts, punishment, training)

THE IMPERIAL COURTS OF JUSTICE OF MISTRESS

Judgement in the Case: The state versus slave......

Given: , **Two thousand and Thirteen**

The case: slave…….. is a slave owned by Mistress He was guilty of ejaculating without the permission of his owner. He was judged guilty of this crime on the 3rd of November 2011, and was sentenced to a fine of £1000.00 (paid) 300 strokes (given) and **to be confined to total chastity with no permission to ejaculate (except when required by his partner) for 6 months.** This was considered to be a grave failure of his obedience and submission to his owner.

The Judgement: Judgement was pronounced by the court on the 3rd of November, 2011 and reviewed in 2012 and at that time the time in chastity was increased to last until at least the 28th of July 2013. The court is now reviewing all Judgements made in 2011 and 2012. The slave ……… is therefore to be returned to the court for consideration of whether an extension of his sentence to chastity should be applied.

In addition there is evidence of further wrongdoing and failure by the slave which needs to be taken into consideration.

Including: not being appropriately dressed, showing Her disrespect and the wilful decision of the slave to prepare his nipples before attendance without orders risking discovery.

The Judgement

he is to stay in chastity for a further year only to be allowed sex when his partner wishes it. he is fined £1000.00 which must be provided within 7 days. he will be punished on three separate days between June and September. Mistress has decided and said "you will not like the punishments". he is not to know them in advance. These are punishments and not fun: these are not going to be pleasurable. his fate is sealed.

Mistress ………… is authorised and requested to use "All Necessary Measures" to ensure that slave………. remains obedient and submits to Her

THIS IS THE ORDER OF THE IMPERIAL COURT AND NO APPEAL IS ALLOWED FROM THIS ORDER

It is right for Mistress to punish her slave for failing Her. It is there both to punish and to remind him to be more mindful of Mistress all the time. he must concentrate on every order She gives. Mistress rules slaves mercifully but firmly.

J is for Jewels

Jewels and the Mistress

Mistresses look good in jewels and nice things but sometimes the jewellery they wear says more than is obvious to the passing observer.

They may wear a brooch or pendant that is special to them; that shows their slaves who is boss. A dragon brooch, a specific design, mini handcuffs, can all be used to make the point that here is a powerful person. The Mistress may also wear a key as a pendant around her neck. She knows it is the only key to the slave's chastity or collar; no one else knows. When the slave sees the key hanging there he knows She is making a point; She is in control and holds the key to his life.

Other Mistresses like to wear bracelets or bangles which carry the keys to their slaves.

Jewels and the slave

Most men are not into wearing jewellery, chains around their ankles or wrists or a chain around their neck. They often have their nipples or other parts pierced without good reason.

But a slave may be required to wear locked ankle chains and wrist bracelets of chain, and to have a chain around the neck from which hangs a dog tag with mistress's logo or mark upon it and states that he is a slave, even if it is usually hidden under his clothing..

Mistress may want the slave to have his nipples pierced and bangles hung from them, or his belly button pierced or even more intimate parts. They can all be adorned with items the way Mistress wants it.

Mistress can expect her slaves to gift Her jewels for her adornment, but they will wear Her marks and chains and jewellery to proclaim that She is their ruler and they are the slaves. Of course some slaves will be tattooed to show they are owned as a slave as well.

(See also: branding, bondage, chains, loyalty, nipples, piercing, ownership, tattoos)

K is for Key holding

When a slave agrees to go into chastity he hands himself over to his Mistress and She accepts that control. When he agrees to wear Her chains around his ankles She holds the key.

When i hand over the key to my chains or more importantly the chastity i am taking a big step. This is not play but it is for real. i will not have control of when i am released or how long i will stay locked up. This is massive transfer of power from me to Mistress. It feels so wonderful to hand over that control to my Mistress but it is also deeply scary for now there is no backing out. Scary but right as i am a slave and She should hold all the keys.

When i see Her wearing the key hanging around her neck i really know that i am Her slave. That is just how it is going to be. For me it is rarely as simple as this as i have a life outside where i cannot wear the chastity 24 hours a day so i still have to keep a key to take it off for night time in bed. But then it is replaced with a butt plug so i am controlled 24/7. When i am away from home it is for real, and Mistress has the key and has provided the lock to make sure that there are no spares loose. If i have to go through airport security i am allowed to put on the chastity only after i have gone through, but the lock i have has no key so the slave is totally locked up with no release until i meet Mistress.

For many slaves it is different as they have no need to be released ever except at Mistress's decision. They are totally locked up 24/7. They will have trained with the chastity to check they can wear it for long periods but in the end they will have agreed a chastity contract which hands over the key and the control.

For the key holder there is so much power and for the first time proper control over someone else. They will often find the knowledge that they are now in control so heady and exciting. They can have as much sex as they wish and the slave can serve them as often as they want; the slave will remain locked away with no sex again until they decide and this could be days, weeks, or even months. It has all been agreed up front and is part of the chastity or slave contract but it is still a shock to the slave when he realises this is for real not play and he will be getting no release.

Key holding is such an important part of both chastity and slavery and can be so good and exciting for both partners in this. It means the male is dependant on his Mistress and key holder so She can use this to steer him into good practices of diet, weight, exercise, doing the household chores and cleaning, learning to serve her personally and anything else She wants. They need to have discussed the range and scope of his duties before lock up but once it is in place She can always add in other items. If he whinges and wants release the time can be prolonged for as long as She decides.

But there are times when any male needs to be released. If sores develop the slave is at fault as he has not kept to a good enough cleaning regime, but he may need the device removed to let them heal up. If he has to go for a medical examination he may need his chastity removed in advance, though doctors and nurses have seen so many things that most would not be put off by having a client in chastity.

If he has to fly he may get through security with a plastic chastity device and a numbered plastic lock, but even here with modern systems this could be a problem so it is probably best to let him out of the device, and to put it on once he has gone through security.

If the slave is away for some time then he may need to be inspected, by Skype, or by providing a photograph of the chastity in place plus a same day paper to prove the picture is contemporary to show he is still locked up. If the key used is a numbered plastic lock then the number will show that it has not been tampered with at all.

Otherwise the chastity device can be left on all the time.

But what can men who do not have a Mistress or partner who holds their key do. There are professional dominants who offer key holding services. The man provides the chastity device. The controller provides the lock without a key or a numbered plastic lock. The man pays for this service, provides evidence that the lock has not been tampered with and receives the key when his time is completed. This can then be used to develop him further with tasks to be performed whilst locked away, evidenced by photographs. It can be a good way for a man to be trained to prepare him for service to a real Mistress or partner. But it is not the same as having a partner close to you who has the key and the control as part of a whole life.

For the man who wishes to experiment it is possible to leave the key at work, or with a friend in a sealed envelope, or post it so it will arrive in a few days. Of course if it gets lost in the post then there is a problem but most locks can be removed with a hacksaw and lots and lots of care.

Handing over control of your chastity device or anything else to be locked away is such an intimate act that it changes the way the man sees both himself and his key holder. It can be the open door to submission and slavery to start on that path, or an integral part of living life as a slave. i am so glad that Mistress is my key holder. It helps to hold me in the slate of slavery i crave.

(See also: chastity, chastity contracts, contracts, chains, power exchange, domination, ownership, power of the Mistress, reality, remote control, training)

K is for kicking

Mistress holds all the aces when it comes to striking a slave in bondage. He cannot move and She is free to hit and strike any part She chooses. She can spank him, paddle him, cane him, use a crop a flogger or a whip, or just pummel him with Her fists.

She can also use her feet to crush him, to prod him and to kick him. This is hard to take as the blows can do damage so needs some thought in advance and agreement form the slave as to how and how hard he can be kicked. A kick in the ribs can break them. Kicks to the balls can bruise and destroy them by causing severe bleeding. Kicking can easily cause bruises which will be present for days and fade to a variety of colours, purple, brown and yellow before they disappear.

So kicking to cause bruising is not a good idea if the person being kicked will be seen unclothed at home or work in a changing room and would not be able to explain their bruises. Many sports lead to bruising because of direct physical contact so this can often be used as an explanation.

But a Mistress may enjoy kicking her slave and the slave happy to be kicked, even in the balls which can be very, very painful. So as long as there is a little care not to cause real damage and it is agreed in advance as being within limits then kicking slaves is yet another way in which a Mistress can show Her power over Her slave, punish him, and make him realise who truly holds the power. Mistress has kicked me in the past and i found it painful but She prefers to use Her hands, Her floggers, and Her electrics to torment me and punish me. Perhaps this may change; i wait Her decision.
(See also: caning, crops, flogging, paddles, punishment, tawse, training, whips)

K is for Kidnapping (agreed in advance)

When a man is kidnapped in the real world it is totally shocking. He is grabbed, hooded, taken away and has no idea what will come next. He might be held for ransom, tortured or killed. The physical and mental shock is extreme. But that is the risk of working in many of the world's trouble spots. To prepare people going to work in such places there are commercial "Hazardous Environment " courses which prepare them for the risks they must face and help them when they are making decisions on what to do or where to risk going. Often these courses incorporate a "kidnapping scenario" at the beginning to shock the participants and remind them of the risks they will face. Being prepared for such a risk allows them to cope with the shock of a kidnap attempt, and may allow them to escape, or cope better when held captive.

"Kidnapping" in the context of BDSM is different. There is agreement in advance that the slave wishes to experience a kidnap scenario. he knows the outline of what is to happen and he knows that he is safe and this is play not reality. Yet it is very intense all the same. he may have agreed what may happen to him, and where he is to go for the "kidnap". He has agreed how far the play can go and how long he may be held.
But when he is suddenly grabbed, pushed into a car or van and hooded and secured with handcuffs or plastic ties it all feels totally real.

Once secured and in the dark the kidnapped slave can be driven around for a while to disorientate him and then taken to where he will be held. The greatest risk is that someone in the street will see the snatch and think it is real, phone the police, give the car number and start a hunt which will lead to disaster. Where the kidnap occurs and how it is done needs to be thought out and done where no one will notice anything suspicious.

The slave can then be taken somewhere secure and held, hooded and in bondage and played with by his captor or captors. He can be left in the dark, exposed to stress positions and loud noises, shouting and threats, and tied to a chair for interrogation or beating. He will have no idea of what is coming next and it will be very intense. At the end he will need to be released and will need a period of coming down from the experience, and quiet sitting and relaxing before he should go back to "normal" life.

Often it is best for there to be more than one captor; one to drive the car or van and one to make the snatch. The place he is taken may already be known to him but hooded and confused with all that has happened he may not even realise that
This means that a Mistress can get her friends involved in the whole enterprise and all of them can have a lot of fun, preparing for the kidnap and carrying it out.

If the slave has discussed a Kidnap with his Mistress or someone who enjoys this activity then he will have agreed things in advance. He can be sent to somewhere he does not know and given a series of orders by phone or text to confuse him, until he is steered to the site of kidnap. He may know the voice of the person he has been communicating with but the person who does the snatch may be someone different, so this will confuse him further. The line between playing and reality will begin to blur very quickly. If he is also taken somewhere he does not know, left tied up in a garage or cupboard and then pulled out to be abused, threatened and interrogated it will all seem very real. He will only really grasp that it was all fun after the ordeal is over.

There are some professional dominants who offer kidnap as one of their services. They will agree limits and duration in advance and require paying in advance too for their time. It is always important to discuss things fully before agreeing to anything so the slave does understand and gives fully informed consent to all that is going to happen.

i have been subjected to a kidnap ordeal only once. i had discussed things with my Mistress and She wanted to try it. i did not know but two of he friends were to be involved as well, one of whom i had never met.

i was sent out from her house to get some shopping, then approached from behind and grabbed by someone i did not know at all. Then i was hustled onto the floor of a car with a pillow case over my head and plastic ties to secure me. i was driven around for what seemed like hours, and had no idea where i was going or how long it had taken as i lay there on the floor in the back of the car held down by the legs of a kidnapper.

Once they had had their fun the car stopped and i was required to keep my eyes shut and the bag was removed. i was marched into a house by two kidnappers and up the stairs. Although i knew the house well i did not realise it was Mistress's house i was being taken into. i was in a state of shock and confusion that prevented me thinking or examining my situation. It was life in the moment. The bag over my head was replaced to cut of all light and i was secured to a garden chair to be slapped, taunted and questioned. It was so intense.

Only when the hood was removed could i see the smiles of the three kidnappers in front of me and realise that this most intense experience had been fun for all of us, but particularly for the kidnappers. It had lasted only just over an hour but felt much longer. It could of course had there been time have lasted a night or even a whole weekend. i wonder when Mistress and her friends will want to kidnap me again and what ideas they will have to make it even more intense and fun for all of us.

(See also: bondage, blindfold, darkness and disorientation, isolation, sensory deprivation,)

L is for Latex

Latex rubber provides sheets to lie upon and to wrap up a slave so he is helpless, bags to use to imprison him and can be used to make collars, cuffs and in strips to hold him down not able to move.

Latex sheeting can also be turned into clothing which fits like a second skin. It can be made in any colour and can be placed on any part of the body. The slave can be placed in latex socks, tights, pants, shirts or hoods or in any latex item of clothing and if this is how Mistress wants him to look then this is what he will wear.

Latex fits tightly like a second skin so a slave or Mistress in latex will be tightly cocooned in the latex. In Mistress this will show off Her physical attributes. In the slave it will hold him tight. But there are problems. A latex garment is not able to breathe so sweat builds up underneath it. The slave may have difficulty putting on something that is tight and only slightly stretchy, and also have difficulty getting it off. Garments are often thin so they can easily rip and cannot be repaired so it is often a good idea to use a lubricant or spray to make it easier for the material to slip over the skin.

Another problem is that a slave in rubber or latex loses a lot of their control of temperature. If the environment is hot he will get very hot indeed, sweat, and almost "cook in his own juice". This is a particular problem if he is put in a body bag and left for a period. Similarly if it is cold he will become very cold quite quickly and this may make it more difficult for him to cope with prolonged bondage or anything else being done to him.

One advantage of latex, however, is that it can be made into garments of multiple layers which can be inflated. The slave can be in a bag gradually inflated to increase pressure upon him until he can hardly breathe or put into an inflatable hood which turns into a tense rubber ball with only an air hole for breathing. Latex is also used in vacuum bags then they can be evacuated of air with a suction pump so that the slave is vacuum packed. So a slave can be crushed with pressure or vacuum packed.

i like it when Mistress puts me in the inflatable bag or hood. The pressure is so great and Mistress can use the inflatable bag as a seat or sofa to recline upon. The bag also has holes closed with flaps so She can still torment any part of me even when i am helpless and crushed in the bag.

Latex clothing comes already made and there are many companies which make standard sizes of clothing or can create new costumes which can be colourful, bizarre and spectacular with areas of skin peeking through the latex, or wings, protuberances, and a strange appearance likely to shock and awe.

Many Mistresses are happy to cope with the difficulty of getting in and out of the latex costumes and difficulties with temperature control because they like the designs and they feel good in latex. Mistress looks wonderful in leather but She also has a custom made latex cat-suit in black and gun metal grey with an integral corset and bolero jacket. In this She looks totally spectacular.

Latex can also come in liquid form in pots ready prepared and applied directly to the skin. A complex multicoloured costume can be created directly onto the skin though hairs that do get caught up in the material as the latex dries do get pulled out when it is removed. Most creations require 3 or more layers, each allowed to dry which can be hastened with a hairdryer. The more layers the thicker the garment and the longer it can be worn. But it can be worn all day, you can go for a swim in it, and it can look most spectacular, but hours of preparation are needed to get such a result.

Some people of course are allergic to latex and it brings them out in a rash. Even latex kitchen gloves can do this so for these people latex is not on.

(See also: body bags, collars, cuffs, hoods, leather, pressure, rubber, vacuum packing)

Leg Irons

When handcuffs are attached to the ankles linked by a short chain they are called leg irons. They keep the slave from separating their legs and act as a hobble. The slave in leg irons can only walk around with short steps.

If the leg irons are attached to a firm anchor point then the slave is immobilized and cannot get away. If the leg irons are attached to hand cuffs and a collar or waist chain the slave can be kept limited in what he can do. If the leg irons are attached to a short chain or cord around the balls then the slave is forced to keep his legs bent and cannot straighten them without producing severe pain.

Mistress uses heavy manacles as leg irons on me, limited with a 50cm chain. When i walk around i make a clanking sound as i do so. This is because She likes to hear me when i clean Her house wearing a shock collar around my balls as well so She can shock me if i am slow

(See also: bondage, cuffs, handcuffs, manacles, domestic service)

Leash

A dog is taken for walks on a lead or leash and a slave can be leashed by his Mistress. She may want to place a collar around his neck or attach a leash to his collar. She can drag him around standing or on all fours like a dog.

This can include taking him for walks outside though here the lead is often run down the arm under a jacket to emerge at the wrist so the leashed slave appears to be walking hand in hand with Mistress but in fact has his lead in Her hand and is held under Her control. This is invisible to outsiders but obvious to the slave.

Being leashed and lead around by Mistress shows Her power over the slave. She is in control. She has the power and he will go where She wants. She pulls and he follows.

When Mistress wants to show She is in control over me as Her slave and property She will clip a leash or a choke chin to me. When She pulls i have no choice but to follow. It is powerful reminder of Her power and control over me. i am not free to move as i want because i am a leashed slave who follows his Mistress's lead.

It is such fun to be taken out by Mistress on a lead. It looks as if we are walking hand in hand, but the lead is keeping me from walking too fast or too slow and a sharp tug tightens the lead around my neck and nearly chokes me.

(See also: bondage, collar, ownership, training)

L is for Leather

Leather is often used for slave collars, cuffs, and harnesses used to control the slave and to place him in bondage. It can be easily fashioned to make tight cuffs, padded so as not to tear the skin which can be worn for hours or days. Leather straps can hold the slave down on a bondage table or whipping bench to keep him still for beating and other torment. Some body bags are made of heavy leather. The slave is placed in the bag which can be strapped tightly to keep him immobile to be left all night.

Leather is also often used in clothing. Slaves wear leather if their Mistress wants it. If She likes of the slave in leather, whether a leather collar, harness, clothing or whatever She wants he must wear it. If She wants him in a leather corset than this is what he will wear. Paddles and whips and floggers are often made of leather and the feeling of being flogged with a multiple tail leather flogger is amazing, especially if the Mistress uses Her full strength.

But leather is also a material that can show Mistress at Her most powerful. In the 1960's many men would have happily knelt in adoration of leather clad Diana Rigg or Honor Blackman in their extremely sexy cat-suits in the series " The Avengers" on the television. Black leather gives a menacing appearance to the Mistress. A leather cat-suit shows off Her magnificent physique. A leather biker jacket shows Her independence and lack of conformity with societies norms.

But leather clothing has become mainstream. Department stores sell leather skirts, dresses and jackets in all colours and styles. The leather can be black which plays to the dominant appearance. There are just so many options to choose from. Many Mistresses like to wear leather, particularly black leather as part of their "costume". It shows off their domination and their power.

But for the slave the appearance of a Mistress in leather can be a real turn on. Many slaves find the image of a leather clad Mistress really arouses them and sets them off. The fetish of leather means that for some it is only the smell, the texture and the feel of leather that can arouse them at all.

Of course leather is also used for shoes and boots. It is hard wearing, beautiful, takes a shine and shows off the feet and legs. It is also comfortable so that many Mistresses will wear patent leather high heels or leather boots, ankle, knee high or thigh high emphasizing their height, their power and their superiority over their slaves.

i think that Mistress looks fantastic whatever She wears as She is tall, imposing and looks so superior and dominant in any garb. But She looks good in boots and it is privilege to kneel and prostrate myself at her leather clad feet or boots. She looks absolutely the most amazing in Her leather cat-suit which She had made specifically for her. It makes her look so dominant and powerful and 10 ft tall.

For me leather is what Mistress uses to place me in bondage and with paddles, flogger and whips to beat me; but She does look so good in leather, particularly that cat-suit

(See also: bondage, body bag, corsets, cuffs, domination, floggers, latex, power exchange, ownership)

Loyalty

Many men visit professional dominants and go from one to another. However they may say that they are the slave of one, they are cheating in seeing or communicating with other Mistresses.

Seeing how you relate to different Mistresses may be reasonable when a man is starting on the submissive life but if he wants to be a slave then he needs to be loyal to his Mistress.

A slave should be ordered not to communicate with or see other Mistresses even if his Mistress is away for a period. The only exception to this should be if his Mistress orders him to see someone She knows. Now he is obeying Her.

Once i became a slave to my Mistress and She accepted me as Her slave She required me to stop all contact with any other Mistress and banned me from communicating with them.

i was allowed to access sites but only to help Her produce Her own website and get ideas for it. More recently i have been allowed to look at sites for cities we would be visiting so that She could contact those with a similar lifestyle.

Loyalty to one's Mistress means being loyal to Her, waiting for her if She is busy and accepting that She is in control of the slave. If anyone criticises Mistress the slave is there to defend Her. If She has tasks which are difficult for the slave to perform but She needs it the loyal slave will do them.

If She has problems he must be loyal. If She has difficulties he must be loyal. If there is any conflict he must be loyal to his Mistress. For me being a slave has changed into being property owned by my Mistress. She owns me and i MUST be loyal always even to the end of time.

There is no time limit to the loyalty a slave should have for his mistress. It is for life.

(See also: chastity, contract, domination, ownership, power exchange, submission)

M is for manacles

In past centuries prisoners were controlled by putting them in heavy steel bands locked into place with padlocks or rivets hammered on by the local blacksmith. Slaves were transported in heavy manacles to prevent them getting away. Examples of these slave irons and manacles can often be seen in museums.

Manacles made from heavy steel now have a place as a tool for bondage in modern BDSM. Mistress has a heavy steel collar She uses on me which weights over 1Kg in weight. It is bolted into place around my neck and feels so heavy. It is then fixed in place and here will be no escape. There are also heavy steel cuffs for the wrists and ankles each of which is joined by a short chain. i can walk in the leg irons and work in the wrist irons but it is difficult because of the weight of the irons. They are locked with an Allen key which Mistress holds and once they are bolted in place they are totally inescapable. A slave in them knows he has no hope of escape.

Of course the addition of extra chain and a few padlocks can convert the manacles into a system of bondage which leaves me helpless or secured to the wall to be left until Mistress wants me for something else.

(See also: bondage, cuffs, chain, handcuffs, leg irons)

M is for masturbation

Men masturbate because they want to and enjoy it. They look at pornography pictures on the internet or play scenarios in their mind and touch themselves until they have an orgasm. Often this occurs at least once a day even in men who are in a relationship and having lots of sex.

But that is not how it should be and for slaves that is not how it is going to be. A slave hands themselves over to his Mistress to control them and this means that She will control his orgasms and when he is allowed to masturbate.

He may agree to limit masturbation or always to ask Mistress's permission before he does so and some slaves are able to do this on their honour.

But many slaves cannot control themselves and need stronger means employed. This is where the use of a chastity device comes in. Mistress and slave agree that he is to go into chastity and his penis and balls are placed in a chastity device. This prevents him from touching himself and acts to prevent an erection as well. Most slaves locked away in a chastity device can no longer have an orgasm, so masturbation becomes a thing of the past. Mistress is the key holder and She decides when the device can come off. She controls both the man and his orgasms.

Many Mistresses consider masturbation by their slave as a crime and punish severely any slave who does it. If the slave has agreed not to masturbate as part of his slave or chastity contract he needs to have help to do so. Mistress holds the key to his release and that is how it should be.

When younger i masturbated a lot always to fantasies of being dominated, cast into bondage, or abused by a powerful Mistress. Now i live the life of a slave and any masturbation is a crime. When i failed Mistress and had an orgasm which was not sanctioned She punished me; a fine, flogging, 6/12 of total chastity. Now the judgement of the court is that i should stay in chastity with no release for masturbation still and this will go on for another year at least. Mistress will then decide again.

For me any release or orgasm is at the decision of Mistress which is why i wrote this section on a flight to America with my parts locked in a steel chastity device told to apply it once through security, and also to throw away the key. Mistress had the only keys and i had none. Masturbation is now a thing of the past changed by Mistress and her training methods.

(See also: chastity, chastity devices, contract, ownership, power, sex, submission)

M is for Mistress's Mercy

Mistress is merciful when She decides She will give mercy. She may decide to release a slave from an uncomfortable bondage position or stop flogging him but equally She may decide not to show mercy this time. It is Her decision.

She controls mercy; She decides no matter how much the slave may beg Her. If of course "mercy" is the safe word that Mistress and the slave have agreed to use to stop any activity then begging for mercy will lead to cessation of the torment. But it is not the case otherwise.

She will be observing the slave closely and She knows the signs of distress in He slave. If She feels he has taken as much as he can then She will stop even if he has not begged for mercy. It is a mercy that She decides to grant because She is feeling merciful. Of course She can withhold it as well.

i am allowed to beg Mistress for mercy when She is beating me. She knows that i will only do so when i am very close to the limit of what i can take or feel beyond it. Sometimes it is because of other factors, temperature, tiredness, dehydration which make it difficult to cope. But Her mercy does not mean that things will stop. It just means that the point of impact will change or a different implement be used on me. The beating goes on until it is finished even if i beg for mercy.

(See also: contracts, Judgement, ownership, safe word, submission)

M is for mouth

A slave's mouth belongs to his Mistress and She decides when he should speak or keep silent. If She wishes She can gag him or even mute him with superglue. Gagging him keeps him silent when She is flogging or caning him. But if required he can be expected to keep silent for hours or days with no speech at all.

Just as Mistress controls his speech She also controls what he puts in his mouth. She can decide what sort of gag he shall wear or whether there is part of it to reach to the back of his mouth.

She decides what he eats or drinks. He can be expected to eat the food She decides, no matter how unpleasant to eat it and to eat it with his face in the bowl like and animal or allow him implements or even to sit up to a table. She can adulterate the food with added hot chillies fluff, earth, even with cigarette ash or anything else She thinks of and he must eat what he is given. All of it.

Similarly he must drink what he is given . It may be nice or nasty. It may include Her urine either directly into his mouth or collected previously. She can use him as a ashtray to drop Her cigarette ash into his open mouth. Nasty tasting but a slave cannot choose and Mistress may wish it.

The mouth of a slave belongs to his Mistress just like his penis, balls, back passage, and indeed any part of him.

(See also: ashtray, domination, food control, gags, quiet, training,)

M is for Mummification

The ancient Egyptians mummified their dead by wrapping them in layers of cloth bound tightly around the body. This prepared them for the afterlife. Then they were lowered into a coffin or placed in a sarcophagus and placed in the tomb.

Mummification of slaves means binding them in layers and layers of material to render them helpless. The slave is secured and his arms and legs are bound and then layer after layer of material are wrapped around the legs then body to bind the arms to the sides. The head can be covered as well as long as there is a hole through which the slave can breathe. The binding needs to be tight but still allow the chest to expand so the slave can breathe a little. If there are problems a pair of shears is handy to cut the slave free.

Bondage tape which sticks to itself works well as also does cling-film or the thicker saran wrap used for wrapping parcels. If cling-film or "Saran wrap" are used there is no way for sweat to get out so the slave is at risk of overheating. Cotton cloth in rolls can be used as well. One problem is that it is easy to wrap a slave standing up walking round and round as the binding is applied, but then he cannot move his legs and it is difficult to lie him down without him falling down. It may take 2 to lower safely to the ground.

The effect of mummification is to make the slave completely helpless. The same effect can be gained with a body bag or a latex sheet wrapped around the slave and secured with tape or rope. The other problem with mummification is that to look good it takes a long time to do. So if there is a limitation on time in a session the slave will be left mummified for minutes whereas it took hours to get him like it.

My experience of mummification came years ago when i was slave to a Mistress interested in Egyptology. She enjoyed tying me up but best changing me into a facsimile of an Egyptian mummy using cotton and tape. More recently Mistress has tended to use rubber inflatable body bags to the same effect.

(See also: bondage, body bag, latex, leather)

M is for Military

Many Mistresses adopt a rigid military like persona from time to time in dealings with their slaves. They act like a sergeant-major who expects perfection in turn out, drill and that soldiers obey him .This can be emphasised by the way they dress, the way they address their slave and the attitude they take. There may be shouting, hitting and bullying and a requirement for the slave to do lots and lots of press-ups or other exercises or take a stress position and hold it.

Some slaves like this and they enjoy being ordered around as if by a superior officer. In the real military much of this would count as bullying and not be acceptable but it works to arouse slaves who enjoy humiliation and verbal abuse.

i have never desired to have a Mistress who acts in this way. She is my superior and should act as She wants to, not as i might like it. i am Her slave and She acts as She wants to without there being any pre-planned role play scenarios. If She did want to do this i would submit and obey but because She is my Mistress and owner not because She might be wearing military like uniform. She can treat me as She wishes any time.

(See also: bondage, domination, power exchange, role play, training)

M is for medical play

Some slaves like to play at being abused by a powerful nurse figure who can make them squirm. They enjoy being given enemas or medical equipment being used on them.

There are devices to open the back passage, steel rods to insert into the urethra where they pass urine and anaesthetic face masks to fit over their nose and mouth and make it difficult to breathe.

Some like needles pushed into or through the skin or to be threatened with knives and other surgical instruments.

This medical fetish is one way to have fun if both Mistress and slave like it. It can be arousing and scary both at the same time. But it is a role play because none of it is real however real it feels at the time.

There are real risks of damage to the back passage or urethra, bleeding or introduction of infection which can be serious. This needs cleaned and sterilized instruments just as in real surgery or the complications can be horrible.

i prefer to let Mistress get on with whatever She wants. If She wants to put an anaesthetic facemask over my face to control my breathing: good. But if She wants to do something else it is Her decision not mine.

(See also : breathe control, enemas, needles, role play)

N is for nails

Mistress has the most beautiful and lovely nails on both Her feet and Her hands. The feet look so wonderful with their painted nails as i kneel or lie prostrate at Her feet. i am permitted to kiss them and have been informed that i will be trained to give Mistress a pedicure so Her nails are perfect at all times. Such beautiful toe nails are worthy of my foot worship as also from all of her slaves

But Mistress has nails on her hands that are even more spectacular. She has them prepared and coloured by Her manicurist and She also has the edges of Her nails sharpened when She knows i am coming to attend Her.

So once She has me kneeling at Her feet She can rake Her nails up and down my back. She can trace out patterns on the skin and scratch me with Her name to show that i am Hers. She can press the sharp nails into the skin and make me squirm and shake with the pain. The nails can also be pressed into use to torment me anywhere else as well. Two sharp nails pressed together with a fold of skin between them or pushed into the balls can make me squeal.

But the most fun comes when She uses Her nails on my nipples. The edge of the nail presses in. The tips of the nails bite down hard. The nails scratch where the nipple is already most tender. Such pain and pleasure are rare to find. i gaze into Her eyes as i see Her implacable gaze. She knows where She is going to use the nails next but i have no idea what will happen. It is all so very good and shows how She controls all of me and can do what She likes with my body which is Hers to use.

Now She is concerned that my nails are not Ok. If i am ever allowed to give Her a foot massage my nails must be short, well-trimmed and clean. My toe nails are not as good, however so they need trimming and tidying. i have been taken for the first time for a pedicure so the nails have been cleaned polished and finally covered with clear varnish. For the first time i have been given a pedicure, and i had to sit there in my ankle chains with bare feet whilst Mistress discussed with the therapist how She wanted my nails treated. The feet are on my body but they belong to Mistress

(See also: foot worship, nipples, ownership, submission, training)

N is for nipples

Mistress owns my nipples.

Most erotic literature concerning nipples is about women and their nipples and almost nothing is written about what can be done with male nipples.

When i started as a slave my first Mistress used to twist and squeeze my nipples and apply clamps and weights. i discovered for the first time that nipples were full of nerve endings and that they could provide so much sensation. At that time my nipples were very small, normal size for a man so there was little for Her to play with.

She told me that my nipples were too small and She wanted them larger. Her initial solution was to get me to go and have them pierced, but this was not possible for me at that time. So She introduced me to the idea of nipple training , wearing clips on the nipples to make them swell up and gradually increasing the severity of the clamps and their tightness so that the nipples cold remain swollen and start to grow. i followed her orders and wore clips made from hair grips and over time my nipples became larger and more sensitive.

For the past 7 years i have been slave to mistress and for the past two years i have been owned by her as property so now my nipples are hers; they are Hers to play with and torment however She wants; they are hers and i must train them so She can play with them.

This means that every day i must do some training. i must wear nipple clamps for hours at a time, or put rubber rings on my nipples which make them swell up. Each evening i must spend time stretching them and twisting them to improve their state for Mistress.

Now Mistress has decided She wants the nipples adorned from time to time and so She has bought nipple jewellery to put on them. There is a star shape, a sunburst, and rings and they can be held in place with glue. They are hidden under my shirt but they are there to emphasise that mistress owns the nipples and that there are Her possession.

All the training is to provide Her with nipples to play with in sessions. i am still surprised how sensitive the nipples can be and when She does things to them all i want is more, more, more. With all the training something that was so small is now the size of a large grape when clamps are tightened and that means more can be done with them.

When the nipples are clamped or rubber rings are put on them they become very sensitive. If i am blindfolded or hooded and in the dark it feels like there is an electric shock going through me when Mistress even touches the nipples. Clamps can be attached to the tip of the nipple where it is most sensitive or to the base. They can be linked by a chain and weights applied to pull out the nipple still further. When Mistress pulls hard on the chain the nipples feel as if they are going to come off, and they can be used as a lead to guide me around.

Simple touch can be pleasant but i have found that if the nipples are slapped with the palm of the hand, flicked with the finger nails, hit with a ruler or the end of a riding crop the level of sensation rockets. It is both harsh and pleasure at the same time. This is the paradox that for me as a masochist the pain and the pleasure are so combined i sometimes cannot tell them apart.

i find it fantastic when i am made to kneel up and Mistress uses on of her whips on my chest, catching the nipples with each blow. The day after such a session they feel bruised and ever so tender especially as they rub on the inside of my shirt. A good session leaves them sensitive for days.

There are so many things Mistress can use on my nipples, clamps, rings, pegs, surgical clamps, clover clamps, the list and the options are endless. One favourite trick is to hang weights from the nipple clamps and make me do the cleaning. As I move they swing to and fro; sometimes weights of 1-2lb can be used on each nipple and they really pull the nipple out and down.

For me, however, it is best when Mistress uses he fingers and her nails. She has her nails sharpened from time to time so they can pinch even harder and the feeling is so amazing. When She bites my nipples it feels so good. When She stands in front of me and pulls me up onto my toes by my nipples or stretches them whilst squeezing between her nails and twisting they feel like they are going to explode.

Nipples respond to all sorts of stimulus not just touch and pain. Heat and cold are also effective in stimulating the nipple. A slave blindfolded and lying on the floor can have his nipples rubbed with a block of ice. Alternatively Mistress can drip hot wax on the nipple to cover it and produce a little mound of wax. The pain as the hot wax hits the tip of the nipple is intense but so is the pleasure.
One advantage of the hot wax is that it can be applied, scraped off and applied again and again. Hours in the dark not knowing when or where the next drop will fall. It is even possible to take a container of liquid wax, such as a tea light candle after it has had the wick removed, have the slave on all fours and press the container of molten wax against the slave's chest until the whole nipple turns into a block of wax.

It is possible to use electrics on the nipples but it can be dangerous. Electricity can pass through the chest and upset the heart and its rhythm. For this reason electro-stimulation is rarely used on the nipples. i am happy with electrics on my balls, penis, backside and everywhere below the waist but not above.

Static electricity forma violet wand is different. Here the spark passes from the wand to the skin and this can be used on the nipples safely. There is almost no energy involved, but at low power the nipple begins to buzz and at high power there is pain.

There are just so many things Mistress can do to my nipples. They care fun to play with and i can only be glad that Mistress likes playing with them and that they have grown to give her something to grab and twist and torment.

A few months ago Mistress decided that the area around nipples should be shaved. She did not want "Her" nipples to be hairy. i was careful not to cut the skin and it went OK. Now She has changed the rules again and when i go to have my Brazilian wax to penis and balls the nipples are included in the treatment.

My nipples stand swollen, clamped and ready for Mistress to use and abuse. She owns them and all the rest of me as well.

(See also, chains, clamps, crop, electrics, ice, leash, nails, needles, spanking, training, violet wand, wax)

N is for needles

Needles can pierce the skin and cause bleeding and bruising. The hole can introduce infection, and if the needle is not sterile it can introduce it deep under the skin. So needle play is dangerous but some slaves and Mistresses like it often as part of medical play.

Of course if the slave is to be pierced then needles will need to be used, but here the piercing should be done by a professional with proper sterile kit and skin cleaning and with dressings and use of antiseptic cream afterwards until everything is healed

Needle use is scary and requires total trust that the Mistress knows Her stuff and has the right needles, new, sterile, and one use only. But then everything that a Mistress does to her slave requires that he trust Her and that She knows what She is doing.

Needles frighten me but some like them.

(See also: medical play, piercing)

N is for nettles

Nettles grow wild in the hedgerows and all over the place as weeds. If you touch a nettle leaf it releases histamine and stings you. The skin swells and stings and there is a red lump where the leaf has touched. The stinging goes on for hours and the redness and swelling of the skin may last all night.

As long as Mistress can protect herself by wearing plastic or rubber gloves She can protect herself from the stings. But She can brush the nettles over the skin of the slave, marking him with red wheals and stripes and also applying the stinging to his balls and buttocks.

He can have stinging nettles applied anywhere and as many as Mistress has available. They need to be freshly picked or they lose their sting. Mistress used to live out in the country with a good supply of nettles close to her door. She could get them herself ready to use on me, or require me to pick a fresh bunch on the way to Her.

One way to make it most intense was to place me in a cage full of nettles and to turn over and over until i was stung on all sides, or to put me in a harness and push nettles under the straps until i had been stung where She wanted it. i could also be made to keep a bunch of nettles inside my underpants until i was in agony.

The only risk with nettles is that there are some people who react badly and can have a generalised allergic reaction with difficulty breathing and swelling up all over. So first check that your slave is not totally allergic, or try a small sting on a leg first to check it is safe. Never put on the chest neck or face in case there is severe swelling and pain.

Nettles are a "natural" product ideal for tormenting slaves. They can be so intense and the pain and tingling and redness last for hours. Balls stung with nettles swell and remain so overnight at times so they are a severe test for a slave.

(See also: arse, CBT, nipples, torment and torture)

O is for overnight sessions

Time with Mistress always seems to go far too fast. If we spend an afternoon together there is never time enough to do everything She wants to do. So the opportunity to have longer sessions lasting overnight, a whole 24 hours, a weekend or even a week of holiday give the chance to take things further.

If there is going to be a long session then there must also be periods for eating and drinking for otherwise a slave becomes weak and less able to function as Mistress requires. Both Mistress and slave will need to get some sleep, though whether the slave is left comfortable or uncomfortable is the decision of the Mistress. He can be put down for the night tied to a bed, put away in a cupboard, caged, or confined to a box or body bag. He can be in chains and ropes and placed how Mistress wants, but he does need to be able to get some rest. For me one good thing about overnight sessions is to wake in the night and realise i am blindfolded and in bondage and cannot escape and that Mistress is resting peacefully. i will have no idea of time and will stay there until She wakes . Of course i also know She will have left me safely and will be able to respond if i have a real emergency, but calling out when not essential will be paid for in pain and suffering the next morning. If a slave disturbs his Mistress's sleep in the night She will not be amused and he will be punished.

If the session allows time for the afternoon, evening, night and the next day as well then the slave can be got up to serve, to prepare a drink for Mistress or Her breakfast and he must wait for permission to use the toilet, to eat, or drink or to wash.

Mistress will have a good idea of what She wants to achieve with the slave during the overnight stay or longer and will be pacing Herself, not trying to do too much too fast. If She decides to flog him until he cannot stand he will be unable to get Her a meal immediately afterwards. He may have entered the stay with no idea of what will happen, a little like in the situation of a kidnapping by arrangement.

What the overnight stay really gives is time, time for the slave to live fully as a slave, and time for the Mistress to enjoy Herself with a totally servile being to serve Her. It is such good fun and helps in developing a slave .i have managed time for an overnight stay only rarely. i would love to spend more time at Mistress's beck and call and to be Her slave most if not all of the time. An overnight stay gives me the feel of what that might be like.

(See also: bondage, body bag, cupboard, cage, domestic service, kidnapping, ownership, personal service,)

O is for Ownership

A submissive is there to submit to his Mistress and this tends to apply mainly in sessions though it can become part of the rest of his life. Slavery is a state of mind. A slave is here to serve his Mistress, submit to her wishes and to obey Her. He may have agreed a training regime which covers lots of areas of his life and all aspects of how he interacts with Mistress. He will have agreed a slave contract which sets out the parameters of his slave life. He is likely to have agreed a chastity contract and to be wearing a chastity device for which the Mistress is the key holder.

i know that there is a lot of debate about these words and acres of print and large areas of the internet are filled with debates of what is a slave and what is a submissive. i really do not know but for me the definitions i have given above seem to make some sense.

i was slave to Mistress from when She agreed for me to be so in 2007 until late in 2011. There were yearly agreements in writing which were my slave contracts and open discussion of their contents and fully informed consent by me when i signed them.

But in 2011 things changed. Suddenly one day Mistress stated "you are no longer My slave because you are now My property" This is a big step change for me. i still consent every time i am asked to do something and do it. But now it is an assumption in our lives.

Property is something that you own. "My car, My house, My Hi-fi set up". But not people. That is how things were in the bad old days of slavery when people were enslaved sold, and condemned to a life of slavery without consent, both them and any descendants as well. This was the slavery that was abolished in the 19th century and did dreadful things to so many people.

i am property but i do not see it as that. i see it as a stage on my life of increasing servitude and consensual slavery. i am proud that Mistress sees me as Her property and seeks to develop me and train me in new skills to serve Her.

But i still see it as a major step change in our relationship, freely accepted by me which shows the increased power that She now holds in my life.

Of course a Mistress has responsibilities to Her slave to keep him fed and safe and not to harm him. That is even more true for a property than a slave as She would be damaging Her own property and She would not want to do that.

But it does take me away from the life of agreed contracts for slavery, chastity and training as there can be no contract between and owner and Her owned slave. There can be a memorandum of understanding written so that both the slave and his Mistress can put down in writing what they understand is going on, but this is only for a check of the situation and is no longer a contract. So i am now so pleased to have reached the state where Mistress considers me Her property. It came as a shock when She made the pronouncement but it is a true description of what i am and seek to remain.

Memorandum of Understanding by the slave

i am the slave and property of Mistress and She owns and controls me. She will have all power over me and be able to do what She wishes. my role will be to submit and obey. i realise that Mistress will have control over all my parts. i may be kept locked in chastity and She may wish to change the lock so only one key exists and She holds it.

She will be able to apply hot wax to anywhere She wishes and to encase my parts in wax to turn them into a solid block. She may apply heating cream anywhere or ice. She will be able to do whatever She pleases with my back passage, use any plug, for as long as She decides, and apply shocks via the electrics at any time. my balls and nipples are Hers to use and abuse in any way She decides.

Whether i displease her or not i may be flogged, whipped, spanked, or caned as She wants, and left marked and bruised. There is no stopping any period of flogging until She decides. Though i may beg for mercy She will decide whether to change site or continue the flogging as before.

i may be kept in any form of bondage for as long as She wishes, including being kept in the dark for long periods and in total bondage all night when She is resting. When and if we go out in public I will be dressed as She wishes, wearing whatever bondage items either under or over my clothing at her decision. i may be transported in a car boot if She wishes, chained and hooded. When we are outside She will be able to shock me using the external controller which provides shocks to my balls at any time, or the electric box which activates my butt plug. i must be ready to kneel to her in public. i may be gagged to keep silent , or be expected to be silent at Her command.

She will decide all that occurs, and the services She requires and i must deliver these to her standards. Any failure to submit or obey will be severely punished in any way She decides. This is my understanding of my situation which excites me so much. But Mistress will only use this as a guide to what she does, She holds real power over me in all the areas detailed above and in anything else She may decide.

The activities described above have all happened at one time or other in my past service to Mistress. It may be She has new ideas of how She wants to torment me. She is always coming up with new ideas. All the time the level of my servitude is getting deeper and deeper, and this is my desire. i truly love to be the slave and property of Mistress and i delight in being allowed to serve her

(See also: chastity, contracts, domination, power exchange, submission, training)

P is for paddle

A paddle has a firm blade with a handle which is used to make a boat or canoe move forward through the water. The blade bites into the water and it is pushed backward making the boat move in the opposite direction.

A paddle with such a firm blade and a handle can be used to beat the arse of a slave. The blade of the paddle is brought down firmly with a slapping sound and the slave will feel the sting as it bites.

Some paddles are rigid with a handle and blade in a single piece often of hard leather, rubber or wood. The blow can be as painful as any other impact on the backside. Other paddles are more flexible and are more like a strap brought down hard to paddle the slave's arse.

Often when Mistress beats me She starts with spanking with Her hand and then moves on to the use of a rigid or flexible paddle, then to the crop and the flogger but always with the probability over my backside once i am fully "warmed up". It can sting so much and a hard paddling is really painful,

(See also: cane, crop, flogging, punishment, spanking, tawse, whip)

P is for personal services

Slaves can be employed to work around the home and to carry out domestic services for their Mistress. But there are many more personal services that She may permit a slave to carry out as well.

Just as She needs to train Her slaves to carry out domestic services to Her satisfaction, the same is also true of any personal services She may require. Because they are personal to Her any failure by the slave may be considered much more seriously and lead to greater punishment.

Mistress may want her clothes cleaned. This can be considered a domestic service doing Her laundry but hand washing and drying and folding Mistress's underwear is a very personal service for a slave.

Mistress may have feet and legs that become uncomfortable and need a massage. The slave who is allowed to massage the feet or legs of his Mistress needs to know how She wants it done and may be required to obtain teaching videos to watch or even undertake formal training.

If Mistress has to spend long periods at the computer She may get tense or stiff shoulders. Here a slave can be trained to provide a relaxing massage.

If her feet are tender and swollen they need to be elevated, A slave is well placed to be Mistress's footstool and to keep her feet up so She can relax properly. He may be considered as no more than furniture but he is acting as furniture She needs and wants so this is personal service too.

Some slaves may be required to remove hard skin from Mistress's feet, or even to apply Her nail varnish. This is really personal and most male slaves have no idea of what to do. The can be taken to a foot salon to be shown by the technician and made to have a pedicure themselves to show them how it is done.

For slaves who love to worship Mistress's feet an order to carry out a foot massage or pedicure or even to paint Her nails will put them in a heavenly state. Her feet, the object of their duty and allowed to touch them too.

The same can also be true of hands, massaged, cleaning or relaxing creams rubbed in to keep a Mistress's hands soft when otherwise they might develop hard skin from all that time spanking the slave.

Mistress has hair which may need to be shampooed and he head given a relaxing head massage. The slave can be trained to clean her hair and allowed to brush Her hair. But always the personal contact should be not because the slave desires it but because Mistress needs it and wants it.

Mistress may allow a slave to assist Her with Her personal care when She bathes. He may run her bath and use the scents and oils to prepare it for her. He needs to make sure the bathroom is fully prepared for her and there are fresh fluffy and warmed towels. She might allow him to wash Her feet, or Her back but She may wish him to leave her alone.

She may want her bed turned down for Her, Her clothes laid out ready as She wishes, or Her clothes packed tidily in Her case for a trip away.

The slave is only allowed to provide the personal services that Mistress decides. She may not want him to be allowed to carry out any of these tasks only cleaning, domestic services, and other menial tasks. She decides; he is to obey.

She decides and these are all personal matters for Her. The slave has no rights at all only a responsibility to serve. If She wants a specific service He must provide what She wants and how She wants it. He needs training to serve and Mistress will ensure that he is trained, competent, and will hold him to the highest standards.

So if Mistress expects any personal service from me i know it must be done perfectly or else! This all for Her pleasure not mine, though i do so love to serve in any and all the ways She has required of me so far.

(See also: foot worship, domestic service, contracts, ownership, training)

P is for Pervertable

Not all the things used on a slave are specifically designed for the purpose. There are many everyday items that can be used instead. Leather lockable cuffs and hoods and latex wear all cost money but bondage and beating can come at a cheaper price.

Some ringbolts costing less than $10.00 each can provide a place to anchor a slave as well as a cross, rack or wheel. A cupboard under the stairs makes a fine cage. Nettles from the garden are free.

For bondage string, washing line, rope, Velcro straps, cheap plastic sheeting, plastic ties and cling-film all work well. A slave wrapped in cling-film is effectively mummified. A slave trussed up in a plastic sheet is secure. All these items are easily available from supermarkets and DIY stores. If you are going away for the weekend and Mistress wants to tie up her slave a good supply of men's ties and long scarves works well.

When it comes to doing things to the helpless slave the imagination can run riot. Pegs used for the laundry have a real bite and a hanger used for trousers has a clamp on either end that can fit over the nipples as an effective pair of nipple clamps joined together.

Kitchen and sport appliances are really good. A table tennis bat or a squash racket applied to the backside can be painful. Flat spatulas and "slices" from the kitchen make good paddles as do many kitchen implements. It is fun to see how many different things you can use. A slave can be imprisoned behind a mask made from a colander usually used to drain vegetables. A pan placed over the slave's head and beaten with a spoon is painful to the ears and extremely unpleasant.

Electric tooth brushes with vibrating heads can be applied to other places than the mouth. Soap is good for washing but a slave who has spoken too much or has sworn in the presence of his Mistress can have his mouth washed out with soap or be made to hold a bar of soap in his mouth. Unpleasant but effective.

Books can be used to swat a backside and a long ruler makes a very effective paddle. Garden canes can be used as a cane. Rubber bands can be wrapped tightly around parts to compress them or pinged to strike. The only limitation to what can be perverted of household appliances is the wicked and cruel imagination of the Mistress. Almost anything is possible.

(See also: bondage, bondage bags, canes, CBT, corset, nipples, flogging, punishment, zipper)

P is for Piercing

A slave who is pierced with a needle through the skin will run the risks of bleeding, bruising and infection that come from breaking the skin surface. This can be a form of play but it can be more seriously a form of body modification.

Mistress wants a slave who looks and appears as She wants him to be. This may mean food restriction and control, exercise regimes or specific clothing to change his shape. Burt some Mistresses like to have their slaves pierced and fitted with body jewellery as well. For some slaves this is possible but for others with another "home life" it may not be easy or possible. Slaves can agree to have piercing of their ears or to put studs on their face or nose. They may be required to wear the ear rings and studs that Mistress decides.

More invasively they may have nipples pierced so that Mistress can have rings inserted to use in controlling them or have genital piercing and a rod or ring which can be used to secure their chastity device, especially the " Lori " tubes.

As in everything in a slave's life this needs to be considered fully before it happens. The procedure should be done by an expert who can do it cleanly and advise on keeping infection at bay. The slave needs to consider in advance whether there are going to be problems at work or other areas of his life. Both the slave and the Mistress need to give thought of what Mistress wants to do, plan and agree a process which may be as permanent as a tattoo and is not for the short term.

(See also: chastity, nipples, needles, ownership, submission, tattoo)

P is for posture and posture collar

Mistress decides on the posture She wants her slave to adopt. She may want him on all fours all the time, held in place with a humbler. When he stands to receive orders She may want him to stand straight, stomach in, chest out, standing to attention. She may help him by making him wear a corset to keep his stomach narrow and give him exercises and food regimes as well.

Some Mistresses allow their slaves to look at them and to se their face. Others may want their slaves to wear blinkers so his gaze is always faced forward and he cannot see to the side.

A submissive slave may not be allowed to look at his Mistress at all but may always have to keep his gaze down and look no higher than her feet. This shows his submission and her power over him.

Whether the slave is required to keep his head high or bent forward one way to ensure this is to give the slave a posture collar to wear. This is a thick leather or rubber collar or even of steel which fits tightly around the neck. Typically this fixes the slave in a position with his head erect. The collar is uncomfortable if he tries to bend his neck or to turn from side to side. Worn for hours it will chafe and can mark the neck. Overnight wear means the slave will not have a comfortable time but may be what Mistress wants.

Alternatively a posture collar can be created which is built up at the back and pushes the neck forward. The slave will be kept in position with his neck bent in submission. he will not be able to look up and his gaze will be fixed on the floor

(See also: bondage, collar, contracts, humbler, humiliation, ownership, submission, training)

P is for Predicament bondage

Sometimes when a slave is put in bondage he is left in a position of difficulty. Whatever he does he is not to be comfortable.

If he is in a humbler the balls are pulled back behind his thighs. If he remains on all fours he is in discomfort after a while from being made to keep that position but if he tries to straighten his legs it will be far worse. he cannot win. If he is in some fixed bondage with his knees bent up he will be comfortable only if he keeps still, except that he will get cramps which may be severe after a while; he cannot straighten up at all to relieve the cramps.

Similarly if the balls are attached by a short chain to the ankles or collar he is kept in difficulty. If he tries to straighten his legs he pulls on the balls. If he tries to pull up his head in the collar he also pulls the balls. Whatever he does it makes things worse for him, and still the original position is not comfortable either.

Mistress can make it so he has no way of being comfortable and is in a predicament no matter what he does. It is cruel to treat a slave so but it is totally reasonable for a Mistress to do so. Why should a slave expect bondage to be comfortable when Mistress can make it more difficult for him. Mistress will decide.

(See also; bondage, chains, CBT, humbler)

P is for Pressure

Mistress may wish to crush her slaves with pressure by sitting on them or standing on them or trampling them into the ground. She may crush their heads between her thighs.

She may want her slave in constrictive clothing or a corset to crush him from top to toe. But there are other ways to use pressure to torment a slave.

He could be put in a position where heavy weights could be placed on him to keep him still and flat. A suitcase full of books or of bricks will work quite well.

He could be placed in an inflatable bag of latex where there is a double skin with him inside. Air is introduced between the two skins and the pressure begins to build. Eventually he can be crushed utterly hardly able to breathe and then She can sit on the bag to increase the pressure further. His head can be encased in a similar double skinned bag and the pressure pumped up until all that can be seen is a large football shape with a small air hole for breathing.

Another alternative is to put him in a bag which can be evacuated of air with a vacuum pump (vacuum cleaner). Now he can be vacuum packed and unable to move at all so the packing leaves him helpless.

However Mistress applies pressure to me ,whether in the inflatable bag or hood or by sitting on me or by putting me in a corset i am helpless. i cannot move yet i can be kept crushed by the bag or the weight.   This is something that can be used for hours or even overnight and there will be no release or reduction in the crushing until Mistress decides to do it.

(See also bondage, fetish/trampling, body bag, latex, training)

P is for power and power exchange

In the relationship of a Mistress and her slave power shifts to the Mistress. The slave voluntarily consents to give power and the Mistress agrees to take it.

It is a big step for the slave to hand over power. The first time i did it i was very apprehensive yet now it seems so normal and reasonable. It seems right to be ordered to put on my chastity and throw away the key leaving Mistress in control of the only remaining key which can release me. i have to trust Mistress that She will use her power wisely and not allow me to get harmed. i have to know and trust her. So accepting a slave state and the loss of liberty that goes with it is a big step but it is one that every one who considers being a slave should take. Further steps will take you into deeper and deeper slavery and submission and the apprehension does not get less though a slave knows from experience that it is all safe and sane.

But it goes both ways. Mistress needs to be prepared to accept the power, to use it and to use the power She has been freely given. There is no use for the slave thinking he has given up power if the Mistress does not want to exercise it. It is a big responsibility for Mistress to take this power. She becomes responsible for seeing the slave comes to no harm. She becomes responsible for his diet, his exercise, his chastity, and the way he lives.

Many men end up in slave relationships outside their normal home lives because of their desire to submit and hand over power. Many women do not want this sort of power and so say they want nothing of it so the potential slave then seeks the expression of his submissive self and hands over power elsewhere.

But women are superior and when a man to enter a female lead relationship he is handing over power to his orgasms, his money, his life and the future directions of travel in his life.

In sessions a submissive may hand over power for a short period to his Mistress but for a slave there is a degree of permanent handing over of power which is an awesome thing. For property the Mistress has assumed ownership with all the power over the owned slave plus the responsibility that entails.

Yet freely handing over power to another is an arousing thing to do. a slave who has been accepted by his Mistress has entered a new life in which his arousal leads to better service for her.

But of course once power is handed over it comes at a price. Mistress has assumed power and will use it. She decides the tasks the slave will carry out. She decides what will happen in a session and what She will use. She sets the standards for any task She gives him and he MUST obey.

This exchange of power means that She will decide his fate if he fails in anything. She has the power of the judge, the jury and the executioner. She decides the punishments and they are real.

It is certainly so for me. i desire to serve and be the best slave i can but Mistress decides what She wants me to do , and what She wants to do with me. She decides when She will beat me, tease me, tickle me and what services She requires of me.

If and when i fail She judges me and makes sure the judgement is carried out to her satisfaction. i failed in cleaning her house in January and She sent me to be caned. Just and fair.

But being a slave and handing over power brings freedom. i feel more free than at any time in my life. i have the freedom to serve and to obey and to submit. i have sought it. i have desired it, and now i have it as the slave and property of my Mistress.

She has the power. She should have the power; i love that it is so.

(See also: chastity, contracts, ownership, punishment, submission, training)

P is for punishment

The image most commonly seen for punishment is of a slave tied down being spanked, paddled, flogged or whipped by his Mistress whilst She reminds him that he is a worm and has failed Her.

But what happens if the slave likes to be beaten and gets pleasure from it. If he likes to be put in bondage or chained up in a cage or cupboard then these activities are not punishment but form a pleasure too.

If i fail mistress and i have done so repeatedly over the past 6 years She punishes me. First She tells me what i have done wrong which i have not always realised so i know the crime i have carried out. Then She judges me. She decides what She will do.

In some relationships the Mistress has a punishment book in which is written all the faults of the slave and often at the end of the week he is punished because of his failings. Some authors suggest that a weekly maintenance beating should be part of this pattern and a regular part of life for the slave.

Of course slaves are always failings their Mistress in large or little ways. The worst punishment is to be denied contact or access to Mistress or even to be dismissed. i do not know how i would cope if Mistress dismissed me. It is an awful fate.

But once a slave is convicted, and he is always convicted, Mistress will decide the punishment. It is Mistress who decides if the punishment will fit the crime or not. Punishment is not there for any pleasure for the slave but it is to prevent him failing his Mistress again. It is there to change him as well as to punish him.

When i failed Mistress by having an orgasm without permission She gave the judgement. i was fined, given a very large number of strokes , much more difficult and painful than i had expected, and placed in chastity for 6 months. Since then She has revisited the verdict and confined me to chastity for a further 18 months. Her verdict is just and i deserved it.

For failing to clean her house properly i was sent to be caned and this was very severe and painful. i like being paddled and flogged but this was not pleasant at all. The caning left me marked and tender but more important it is something that reminds me to keep the cleaning done to the highest standard.

But more recently She has identified other failings. i have been fined again, i have been given a further year in chastity and i am informed that here will be three further punishments. i am not to know them in advance but they will occur between June and the end of September, and that i am not going to like them. Mistress has decided.

i am apprehensive about them. i worried for weeks before the caning as i was not sure i would be able to cope. Now i worry about what is to happen next. This is as it should be. Mistress wants this to be a true punishment to prevent me failing again. The wait seems long but it is timed top keep reminding me of my crime and the need to behave better and to be more totally focussed on Mistress's needs and orders.

i must prepare myself but more importantly i must change and improve as a slave. i am right to be apprehensive as this is Mistress exercising real power, real punishment.

i need it. Most important of all Mistress has decided it and there is no appeal ever.

So punishment is real and it is there to punish slaves for their failures. It is decided by Mistress and it is not there for pleasure. Each mistress will know what will work best with each separate slave, whether the most severe beating, flogging and caning far worse than anything done with pleasure in mind, restriction of contact or putting in an unpleasant place for long periods, or carrying out tasks and suffering because that is how Mistress wants it.

Punishment is an exercise of Her power and her Majesty applied to her slave and property.

(See also: domination, bondage, cane, domestic service, ownership, power and power exchange, training)

Q is for quiet

One of the most important things about being a slave is being put into silence. There are times Mistress allows her slave to speak and others when She does not want to hear his voice at all.

She can command him to be silent and enforce this taping up the slave's mouth, use of a gag or even superglue to mute him.

But this is an external force to make him silent. More important is the internal silence that comes from being put in bondage and left alone. When i attend Mistress my mind has often been full of all sorts of other distractions, the world, work, etc, all clamouring to be heard. There are just so many thoughts, hopes and fears that it is difficult to become quiet.

Bu i need to become quiet so i can give my full attention to Mistress . i need to be able to be fully mindful of her, the verbal and non-verbal signals that She is giving.
i need to be mindful of HER needs and desires in order to serve her properly as a slave. i cannot do that if i am distracted. So Mistress helps me to go into a state of quiet.

When She secures me in bondage, hoods me, and puts me "down" i am conscious that She is taking control over all my functions. i am left helpless, secured, in the dark, and She goes away so there is nothing to see, little to hear, and no ability to move. i am locked away.

This acts on me to quiet all the internal noise as well. It takes time but when i emerge into the light, blinking and with Mistress's face before me it is all changed. i am ready to serve. There have been times when things have been bad when this has taken up to a couple of hours but it always works. When we have the opportunity for long periods together the external noise stills and i am left fully myself focussed and more mindful and i can concentrate on my purpose in life. i am the slave and property of Mistress . This is what i enter the silence to find is true. The silence within and without join together and i am able to live fully in the now.

(See also: bondage, bondage bag, gags, hoods, isolation, mouth, overnight stay, ownership, power, sounds, training)

R is for rack

A rack was used in torture chambers in the past to stretch out the victims until their joints dislocated if they failed to answer the interrogators questions. In BDSM a rack allows the slave to be stretched out with his hands pulled one way and his legs the other so that he becomes helpless and the Mistress can then do what She wants to him. If he is on his face this makes him ready for flogging, and if he is on his back the nipples, cock and balls are all fully available for the Mistress's fun. The stretch is never taken so far as to damage the slave, but he is in discomfort form the forces that are pulling him out. If the rack is built above a cage there are often holes in the top of the cage so weights can be applied to the slaves balls when he is racked so they can hang down and be stretched on their own.

The only problem with a rack is that it is large and takes up space. In Professional Dominant's chambers a rack may be paced on top of a cage so the slave can either be put in the cage or stretched out on top of it. For use at home a rack would need to be a minimum of 8ft long, to allow the slave to have his arms stretched out above his head. It might need to be longer if the slave was tall and had long arms.

Those Mistresses who want to stretch their slave on a rack might be able to use a commercial chamber for a period of play but few will want to use that much space in a normal home, or have the money for a professional system which may be very expensive.

i used to enjoy being stretched out on the rack so i could not move and my Mistress could do what She wanted with me. But of recent years i have had problems with my right shoulder so it does not stretch out properly. This means that the rack cannot be used to its full potential without the risk of damaging the shoulder. i am not alone in this so if a slave has limited shoulder movement and cannot put his arms straight up in the air then using a rack may not be possible or even safe.

But a slave stretched out on the rack with Mistress able to tighten the cords to pull him out can be a fine sight and a Mistress may want to try it. As long as She makes sure the slave has no shoulder or other joint problem this will work well, and stretching the slave's back may even help if he has back disease by reducing pressure on the back joints.

(See also: bondage, cage, suspension, nipples, CBT, flogging, torment and torture)

R is for reality

Fantasies bring up so many interesting ideas of how to be a slave and what a Mistress can do with him but they are not always practical or fit with reality. Many slaves have a life outside of their slavery which includes a partner and home life so time with Mistress will be limited. Most slaves have a job so they are further constrained though being "at work" can be an excuse not to be home early and a flexible work plan can allow for regular time with Mistress.

But some things are not always possible or desirable. A slave who has a job may be expected to go to work in a collar, ankle chains, chastity and a corset but only if all of this can be hidden underneath their clothing and they do not need to go through security at work.

A slave who has a separate home life may desire to have nipples pierced, be branded or to be tattooed with his Mistress's name but this is not easy to hide and could lead to catastrophe.

Caning can bruise and nipples may bleed and be bruised after a particularly active session and this must be hidden as well.

But there are things that may be possible. A slave may be able to wear a butt plug at night if his partner "never goes there", or to be sent for a Brazilian wax. As long as he is able to look "normal" at home so many things are possible.

But reality also has to apply to what happens when the slave is with Mistress. If there is time then it might seem possible to keep a slave locked away in a cage for long periods of days or longer but how is he to be able to pass urine (? into a bottle or catheterised or connected to a bag) or open his bowels. Mistress does not want a stinking mess in Her cage.

Similarly a slave could be kept without food or water for long periods but he will become dehydrated and weak without adequate fluid, and without food or hydration he can become ill and not be able to cope with what Mistress has planned for him. Of course Mistress defines what he may eat or drink, how he is to approach it, when he is allowed food or drink and this gives Her enormous power over the slave. But he does need to receive food and drink to be able to function properly as a slave. Just because all fantasies are not possible does not mean that the reality that can happen is not amazing. Reality is always better than fantasy because it is true.
.

(See also consent, contracts, ownership, sane and safe, training)

R is for remote control

Mistress can control Her slaves totally when they are in her presence, but She also has a more remote control on them as well. When a slave is in the presence of his Mistress he can be controlled in every way, kept in bondage, required to keep silent, and given tasks including domestic or personal service to do.

But when i am away from Mistress She still controls me from afar. She decides what i have for lunch, cat food and water. She decides that i will wear my chastity all the time out of the house and the butt plug instead at night. She requires me to wear my collar, my ankle chains and my nipple clips and the tight corset under my clothes. She can require me to show myself to Her on Skype to show that i am obeying Her. She expects me to get regularly waxed and to exercise each day to get fit. Her orders control me from afar no matter where She is in the world. All it takes is a phone call or an email and i have tasks to perform. i prepare these reports for Her, do my exercises, and live my life controlled in so many ways.

But remote control can also apply to devices She makes me wear. If i am wearing the shock collar around my balls her controller can give a shock from up to 400 yards away. If She is in a different room or we are out in public i can be shocked. She can share the shocking device at a party with Her friends and pass it around so i never have any idea when i am going to be shocked or by whom. The same system can be used with a wire around the perimeter of a room or garden so the slave cannot leave. If he approaches the wire boundary then shocks get greater and greater. This is designed to keep dogs from straying but it works well with slaves as well.

With the DL systems shocking device attached to a chastity device the control is awesome. The slave can be controlled via a computer link and shocked, his parts vibrated, or made to go onto all fours (the canine option) He can be confined to within a short distance of the computer, or the same room or just the house and if he tries to go out he will be shocked. Once logged in mistress can control him. She may do this without vision or use Skype so She can see what is happening to him whilst he cannot see Her. On one memorable occasion Mistress was controlling me and shocking me in the UK with the DL whilst She was watching the sunset on a beach in South Africa.

Most remote control is psychological with orders for the slave to obey and a pattern of obedience and more and more orders to control ever more of his life. A simple way to control from afar is for the slave to be required to check emails each day at a defined time, and for his daily orders to be transmitted then to be obeyed. The greater the remote control the greater the total control of the slave. For me this is one of the keys to serving Mistress that i am never free but always controlled all the time.

(See also: contracts, domination, domestic service, electrics, exercise, food control, ownership, submission, training)

R is for restraint

A slave can be held still with restraints whenever Mistress wants it. She may expect him to keep still for a flogging or paddling but if it is going to be severe She may want to restrain him as well. The restraint may be with cuffs, chains, handcuffs, leg irons or manacles or by the use of rope skilfully applied so he is helpless. Then She has him as She wants him for Her fun. So much restraint is a form of bondage, but restraints can also be worn when the slave is expected to move around. He can be placed in cuffs, leg irons or manacles to make doing domestic services more difficult or to limit his mobility. If he is placed in the humbler his balls are pulled back behind the thighs and he cannot straighten or stand so must serve on his knees.

He can be hobbled with a short chain or rope so he can only take short steps. All of these methods of bondage and restraint have the intention of making things difficult for the slave to move around or impossible if that is Mistress's desire.

i like any form of bondage Mistress decides to use on me and to be restrained by Mistress is enjoyable. But i am never certain what might come next once i am helpless. If it is night time and i am restrained by being put in a body bag then it is likely that i will be left alone to rest, but i might have been fitted with the butt plug which can give electric shocks at any time and any degree of severity so this is possible too.

But restraint is also a restraint of my mind. Mistress decides what is going to happen and i must restrain myself from making suggestions of things i would like and enjoy. She will decide. i may be restrained from speech either with or without a gag.. She will decide.

i live a life restrained and constrained by Mistress as She uses her power over me . She decides what i may do, what sites i may look at and how i can respond to others. She has the power and is in control and that is how it should be. If i am lucky She restrains herself when She is flogging me, for otherwise She can get into her stride and it can be too painful to bear. She controls herself and me in all aspects, so i live a life restrained at Her feet serving her and under Her control either direct or remote. It is always there and the bonds restrain me and control me for Her

Mistresses restrain their slaves for safety to stop them moving, to make them helpless, and to show their total power.   Restrained is how a slave should be for his Mistress.

(See also: bondage, cage, cupboard, domination, cuffs, flogging, leg irons, manacles, training)

R is for role play

It could be said that being a slave is a role play situation separate from the rest of life but for me it is certainly not the case. i find myself profoundly drawn to the situation of being a slave and having been accepted as a slave many years ago and become the property of my Mistress it ahs passed far beyond any role playing of "slave" and "Mistress". Now the rest of life is more play at home and at work and the central fact of my life is that i am a slave.

But for others the role of slave is much more peripheral in their lives. They love to spend time trying to be a slave, and living the life for short sessions only. That is how i started and it is a good way to discover whether slavery is what you want.

The slave may be considering his slavery a form of role-play and the same can also be true for the Mistress. She may be a lifestyle Mistress where the domination and role is actually who She is but many Mistresses have this as only part of their lives and may be different in other situations.

Within the interaction of the slave and his Mistress there are times when particular roles may be desired. The Mistress may want to play the part of a powerful lady with domestic slaves to cater to her every whim some times and other times may want to be the cruel Mistress who tortures her slaves until they cry.

Many men like the idea of being dominated by a nurse in medical play, a military figure in military play or a schoolmistress or powerful figure who will spank the errant child. It can all be good fun.

But it should always be agreed if there is to be any role playing. If the slave does not know he is to be subjected to a kidnap scenario and what the Mistress wants he will not behave as desired. If the Mistress does not like a particular form of role play or does not want to do it with her slaves then it will not happen. Even if the slave wants it, it is Mistress that decides, and many Mistresses like some roles and do not like others. She is in control so SHE should decide. No questions, no begging, no tantrums, just obedience by the slave. That way any role play is agreed, consensual and designed for pleasure by both but the power is wielded in all situations by the Mistress.

(See also: contracts, domination, fetish, medical, military, training)

R is for Rubber

Rubber and latex come from the rubber tree though they can also be made artificially. Sheets of thin stretchy rubber are termed latex and are good for clothing, bondage bags and hoods and can look spectacular as part of latex costumes. They are impervious to sweat so overheating is a danger, and a slave covered in latex may boil or freeze depending on the environment. There needs to be a good sized air hole for breathing for you cannot breathe through a latex sheet. But the costumes and clothing can be tight and revealing and very sexy so many Mistresses like to wear latex. They may also like to place their slaves in latex to take away their identity or hood them so they lose all their personality and become a simple latex covered slave.

Thicker sheets of rubber are not stretchy but hard and shiny. They can bend and flex and make a good substance for making whips and paddles. A heavy rubber paddle split into thongs makes a loud slap as it hits the skin and can be very painful. Often rubber is also easy to clean so if the Mistress breaks the skin and causes bleeding the rubber paddle or whip can be easily cleaned and disinfected.

Rubber and other synthetics are used for the soles of shoes and these can also be used to strike a slave. He can be imprinted with the mark of the shoe, just like the tread of a tyre.

Leather and rubber are so often used in fetish wear, and items used by the Mistress for herself or to use on her slaves. Some Mistresses like one, others the other, and some both in different situations. A slave may desire to be beaten by a rubber clad Dominant, but it should depend on what She wants not him. The slave may have found that to him rubber is a fetish and he cannot get aroused except when he can feel and smell rubber or even taste it on a gag. Mistress will decide whether this is something She likes and use it or not as She decides. his desires are secondary but many Mistresses will try to accommodate strong preferences in a slave, for it helps them gain the mastery over them and show their power in one area then spread to all the rest.

Hard and heavy rubber can also be used to make collars, corsets, and cuffs which can be secured around the slave to restrain him and place him in bondage.

It is a very versatile product often used on slaves and by Mistresses. My Mistress loves Her rubber whip and i like being placed in the inflatable hood or bag. i used to be collared with a rubber collar but now have been placed in one of steel lined with neoprene instead..

(See also: bondage, body bag, collars, cuffs, corsets, paddles, power, training ,whip)

R is for rope

Rope is ideal to use for bondage. The rope itself can be soft and sensuous, especially if a silken type of rope is used. Alternatively it can be made of natural fibres and be rough and itchy. But most rope used in bondage is made of artificial fibres and can be soft or hard, thick or thin, and come in a wide variety of colours. This means that different colours can be used to produce a pattern on the body of the slave.

The rope needs to be looked after and to be kept coiled and tidy between uses otherwise it rapidly becomes knotted and difficult to use. It needs to be cut into short 20-30ft lengths because using longer lengths it is much more difficult to use and more easily becomes tangled. Once you start with a single length extra lengths can always be added in.

It is easy to carry and in the hands of someone trained in its use bondage can be set up quickly. Japanese policemen used to carry a length of rope to secure suspects in place of the more usually used handcuffs in the west. But when you are learning to use rope it can take time to apply so the slave needs to keep still and be patient and the bondage will then be easier and look better.

It is a good tool for bondage with the risks being that a loop of rope around the neck has the risk of becoming a noose and strangling the subject. If the rope is removed rapidly the skin may be damaged and there may be a "rope burn". If a slave is to be put into complex bondage or even rope suspension there are risks that the rope may become too tight and cut off the circulation so anyone using rope for bondage should consider having a pair of shears to cut the rope handy when they do it.

Rope is very versatile as a way of securing slaves. Simple rope bondage around the wrists or the ankles works to immobilize, or the rope can be used to tie together cuffs already on the slave. Once wrists are tied behind the slave and the ankles are secured the two parts can be tied together to put the slave into a hog-tie position, helpless and unable to move. Rope can also be used to produce a rope harness or to wrap around and around the waist to produce a rope corset which crushes the slave and can be worn under clothes outside.

The slave can be tied to a chair so he cannot escape or attached and spread-eagled on the bed with rope around each ankle and wrist tied to then bed frame. All of these are relatively easy to do, quick to put in place and the rope itself is cheap and easy to carry so useful if the Mistress and slave go away or if the bondage kit needs to be packed away when bondage is not happening.

But rope can also be used to make complex bondage arrangements. In Japanese rope bondage there are many different techniques used to secure a slave. There are complex harnesses, bondage to the arms and the body, rope around the breast areas.
A bondage system can be produced which leaves the slave totally helpless and then secured to a raised point so the slave is suspended in the air.

The pictures in videos and bondage books such as those produced by the rope specialist Midori look spectacular and take hours to produce and to make a work of art. For this sort of Japanese rope bondage, often termed the art of "Shibari" practice is needed. If Mistress wishes to use rope in this way on her slaves then She will need to practice, to study videos and manuals or even to take lessons.

There are professionals who will teach this sort of rope bondage, masters and Mistresses of their art and make it all look easy but they can teach simple techniques relatively quickly and many of the books and videos have a step by step guide of how to do it.

What a Mistress needs is time to practice, a compliant slave, lots of rope and a book to show her how to do it. Soon She will not need the book and make the patterns herself. Suspension rope bondage is a different matter for her the last thing a Mistress wants is to string up her slave and have him fall or damage himself.

my experience with rope bondage came first from a Mistress who liked it and used it on me all the time. A subsequent Mistress bought one of Midori's books and used it to guide her with me blindfolded so i could not see what was happening. my Mistress now had the opportunity to study rope bondage with a master of the art when we went to Denver a couple of years ago for a week. We attended classes with others and also with the trainer, just the pair of us. i was the subject and responsible for tidying up the rope afterwards and coiling it away. Mistress learned to put me in a body harness, a whole body harness involving head to toe, a rope corset, and to bind my arms tightly together in many different ways. i was introduced to the difficulty of coping bound sitting with crossed legs arms secured to ankles and head bent forward and other stress positions. It was a fabulous introduction to rope bondage techniques.

Since then Mistress uses rope when She wants to and uses it to make things difficult for me. i may be in a bondage bag but it be made even tighter with coils of rope drawn tightly around it. i can be put in a hog-tie position so i lie on my face with arms secured to ankles behind me , or on the floor with thighs bent so i cannot get up. She uses the rope to link other cuffs and also has had me tied tightly to a chair, ankles to the front legs, back with coils around my stomach to prevent me getting up and with extra rope on to my collar to hold me bending forward. A good position for typing and ideal for Mistress to place me to write reports and do part of the A to Z guide. i was left tied in place for several hours.

 (See also: bondage, cuffs, chains, bondage bag, handcuffs, leg irons, training)

Safe and Sane

There are so many ways in which a slave can be damaged in the sorts of activities that a Mistress and her slave carry out. There are risks which are physical but equally important are those which are psychological or which affect the slave and the community in which he lives.

The motto for BDSM living is often quoted as safe, sane and consensual. Consent is fundamental to everything that happens. Both the Mistress and the slave need to give full consent to their activity. If the slave does not understand the risks of what he is getting into he cannot give consent. If the Mistress does not realise that the slave has a problem such as claustrophobia then She may put him in a heavy hood and he may freak out. Both Mistress and slave need to know what they are doing and make sure things are safe. Only then can there be consent.

If the Mistress pushes the slave into things he does not feel happy to do then She is abusing him. If the slave persuades the Mistress to do something She is not happy to do he is abusing Her. The difficulty comes in the middle of a session when the Mistress is fully engaged and wants to push the boundaries a little and the slave is so hyped up on all the adrenaline and endorphins that all he wants is more, more, more.. Then is the time when things can go badly wrong and the slave be damaged, or find himself pushed out of the play into much darker territory.

So consent comes first, and continuing consent is essential throughout the session or the games Mistress and slave are playing. It comes from understanding and also from trust. A slave who has been the slave to a Mistress for a while has a close relationship with her. She knows him. She knows his capabilities, his endurance, the things he likes and the things he cannot cope with.

he knows Her favourite ways and knows that even when he is fully in a session She will protect him and prevent him coming to harm. He knows that She is experienced in what they are doing. Problems can come when they are trying something new which neither have tried before so then is the time to take things slowly.

Physical harm is always a risk. If there is impact play then the whip or paddle or any other item being used to beat the slave may cut the skin or cause bruising. A cane applied with full force will mark and can scar. In bondage anything tight around the neck can affect the breathing and rope around the neck can cut off breathing all together. If ropes or other bondage items are extremely tight they can cut off the circulation and cause harm or press on nerves and damage them. Anything which damages the skin, branding, tattooing, needles, or piercing can introduce infection which can range from mild to severe or even life changing with HIV and other serious infections

If a slave is to be suspended upright he needs to be watched because he may faint. If he is upside down this is even more likely and an unconscious slave is at high risk of dying. If the suspension is not secure then he may fall from a height and break bones or even his neck. Slaves who are gagged are at risk of vomiting and inhaling their own vomit and should never be left on their own. Electrical stimulation above the waist can lead to irregularities of the heart which can be very serious indeed.

These are all real physical risks which will be considered by the experienced Mistress or slave no matter how enticing an idea for bondage or other activity. They will both need to understand the risks before they try something and be prepared to stop. For rope bondage a pair of shears to cut the slave free of the rope if it will not come off may be essential equipment. But that is no reason not to try lots of things, and to do so carefully. There are risks in anything we do but care and forethought will prevent most of them.

The physical risks of BDSM activity can be more easily seen than the psychological risks to both Mistress and slave. There is a need for trust and this can grow into dependence in time. The slave becomes dependant upon his Mistress in so many ways because it is Her who is controlling him. This can feel very good and act as a release from tension in a slave who lives a busy and stressful life. But it puts a large burden upon Mistress. he is handing over control and She has picked it up. They have agreed this so there is consent. But She may not realise how vulnerable a position this is for the slave, and how much he may need protecting from himself. He may want to do things that are dangerous and She must stop him. he may feel high from all the activity during a session but have a drop in mood afterwards. he may be anxious or depressed. he may have things in his past that come out and cause him distress of which the Mistress has no idea. The more intense the session; the more intense the whole relationship; the greater the risks.

Mistress may also have issues of her own which can be exacerbated by her dealings with her slave. We are all complex individuals with much in our past which can affect the present. In an intense Mistress/slave relationship all emotions are possible both good and bad. This is dangerous emotional territory. One simple situation is that the slave may feel that his Mistress feels more for him than is actually the case. he may want to become her lover. This is not what She wants and it is easy to get into a complicated situation where he may think one thing is happening and it is not so for the Mistress. It is really no different than the situation in any other relationship in life, but the power and the power exchange with Mistress can complicate things and make it more difficult to go forward.

There is another area of safety which is very important. That is the outside world. It may be OK for a slave to be kept in a chastity device a collar or a corset all hidden under his clothing but these are things which might go down badly if his work colleagues found out. If he is taking time off work when he ought to be at work he needs to be careful that these are accepted absences otherwise he may get into trouble.

If he is out in public with Mistress even if both are dressed conservatively and there is nothing to suggest he is a slave and She is a Mistress both may meet acquaintances who know nothing of what is going on with them and may tell other friends or put things on "Facebook" or "Twitter" if they see something untoward. A slave kneeling to his Mistress in public is at risk unless both are certain that there is no one around who knows them to notice. Opening doors for Mistress, carrying her bags etc all look OK but being lead around on a lead may be a step too far. It all depends on where they are and if they are far away from "home "more may be possible. But it is always necessary to be careful.

Many slaves have a complex life. They are slave to their Mistress, have a life of work, but also have a family and home life separate from their slavery. This happens when the slave seeks submission and slavery and does not find it possible at home so seeks it elsewhere. Here it is vital to keep the two lives separate. If the wife or partner at home were to suspect anything then disaster would occur. The slave would be unmasked and the whole web of relationships would fall apart. The wife or partner would be unlikely to understand what the slave was doing and would think they were having an affair. Even though most slaves have no sex at all with their Mistress and may be in a chastity contract where the only sex they get is when their partner initiates and also no masturbation this would be difficult to explain to an angry partner.

So safety demands a degree of care and compartmentalisation. The slave needs to be reminded to keep the relationship of servitude to the Mistress and not to try the same things with the partner. i got into trouble with Mistress when i started to kneel to kiss my partner's feet occasionally. Mistress rightly thought that this was inappropriate and risky as i was beginning to confuse my position at home with my servitude and was more likely to let things slip out. Mistress works very hard to keep me safe in every way.

The slave and the Mistress need to be so careful to make sure that there are no marks which can be seen and the slave questioned about at home. If the slave is going away on business then he can be marked but they must have faded before he gets back. Branding, piercing and tattoos are difficult to hide and impossible to explain. At the end of a session the slave may still be in such a slave state that he may fail to take precautions, making sure no smells on his clothing or in his car, cleaned so there is nothing to see, making sure that his chastity or collar are not found or the tights that his Mistress makes him wear for that could lead to bother at home if found out.

Here the Mistress is protecting the slave from himself. She is making it possible for him to cool down at the end of the session and get his bearings. She is helping him to keep always in context. It is not easy to make sure the three lives of home, work and slavery can co-exist at the same time but it is possible but only with the help of a caring and careful Mistress.

One other situation of considerable risk is if the Mistress and slave go out to BDSM parties where they do not know all the other players. There could be mutual friend of the slave's partner or the slave who might identify them and this could be a bad idea. Going to groups far away from home is possible but even there general care is need to make sure information does not leak.

Mistress and slave will be in touch with each other so there is always a risk of emails being seen, mobile phones being read and what is going on being seen by the partner. This requires care and carefulness, both in how and when communication occurs and on what computers it is done. There should be a separate email account for the slave and the rest of his life and similarly for the Mistress. Text messages should be purged from the telephone and no parcels of "fetish wear or toys" to arrive at the slave's home directly where they can be opened. If he has an Amazon account he will need to make sure any books and other things go to another address and when his partner opens his account this is not apparent.

Once the partner begins to suspect things it is difficult to hide so the best rule for safety is to make sure it does not happen. It is hard to do and requiring care every day but a failure in security can be as disastrous as for a spy being unmasked when operating in a foreign country

As to sanity it is difficult to explain to an outsider why for a slave being flogged and tormented by his Mistress feels so right. There are times and countries and societies where any expression of BDSM is considered a sign of psychiatric disease. Even here and now any fetish wear or appearance may be considered a sign of disease, exhibitionism by some who are very conservative in their thinking, or that something is wrong inside for a man wanting to dress in women's clothes. Even now with so much fetish wear part of the mainstream full on Mistress and slave appearance is unusual and may get commented on.

Sane in this context means that there has been thought before things are done. They are activities that both want to do and no one else is involved. They are secret and will not offend anyone. They are safe and safety precautions have been taken to make sure there will be no harm. They may not be seen as sane by everyone but they are reasonable in the context of the slave/Mistress relationship, thought out, safe, and there is full consent from both parties.

This is safe and sane activity for the Mistress and her slave.

(See also contacts, corset, domination, fetish, ownership, safe word, secret, training)

S is for Safe word

A safe word is a word used by a slave in sessions with a Mistress which means that the slave is unable to carry on and wants to have the severity of any torment reduced or just stopped and bring the session to a stop. he uses a word which he is unlikely to use during a session or one that is generally used in BDSM circles and which is also known to his Mistress. "Yellow" is often taken to mean "this is too severe for me to cope with" and "red" for "STOP NOW" but the Mistress and slave may agree any phrase or word to use for this purpose. .

The purpose of the safe word is to allow a measure of safety for the slave in case he cannot cope with what is being done to him. If the Mistress gets well into what She is doing and gets carried away with Her flogger it allows him to call a halt before he is harmed or damaged. It is a way to keep safety in mind and prevent harm and damage to a slave.

But there are always problems with any stop signal. The slave may get carried away in the moment and want more and more and more and here the Mistress needs to keep a cool head and consider his safety and stop before he is injured, even if he wants Her to go on. If he is trying to impress his Mistress or someone whom She has sent him to for a caning or beating he will not want to use the word and may get more than he expected. That is his problem for he has not used a safe word.

It is there to keep things safe and sane and to prevent damage and works well in most cases.

When Mistress is beating me i know that She knows me well and knows how my body and mind react to what She does. If She thinks She has pushed me over the edge She will often change the site of beating and reduce severity before i get the need to beg for it to stop. Her observation of and knowledge of me means that i can trust her with my body and know i will be safe.

We have agreed that if i beg for mercy this is only because i am at the edge of what i can take, and so then She changes tempo, severity and site of a flogging and carries on. If i cry out that i am unable to take any more She will stop. Neither of these will bring the session to an end but they change what she may do next. There are always different things She can do with me which might include making Her a cup of tea or doing some cleaning. The control continues even if the pain stops for a while.
For us this seems to work. Others use a more formal safe word and that works for them.

(See also: consent, contracts, domination, ownership, safe and sane, training)

S is for secret life

Life is full of risk and private activity may need to be kept private to prevent problems. There are few slaves and Mistresses who are able to live out their lives in public because of potential problems at work and with friends and family.

This is an activity which many in the vanilla community would consider bad, even though they might practice a little bit of mild bondage and some role play in their own sex lives.

The slave and the Mistress need to keep their secret life away from the prying eyes of employers who might not know how to cope. They might accept someone with chains, chastity, and collar and corset under his clothing if they knew nothing about it but if it became open knowledge he might have problems with his job and employment.

Friends and family might not understand and it might blight relationships there as well. Even if the slave and Mistress were married to each other and living together family and friends might not understand him kneeling to be Her footstool at a dinner party, or openly wearing a collar and lead or spending his nights locked in a cage or cupboard. If there are children in the house secrecy becomes even more important.

There are websites for the BDSM community and fetish world such as "fetlife" and there are groups within this with almost any interest from the common to the rare and esoteric. Even there a slave and Mistress might want to be careful in case they find a work or family colleague unexpectedly.

"Twitter", "Facebook", and other social media sites mean that anything you post there goes open to the whole world so a picture of a slave in latex and chains will embarrass him and show his interests to friends and relations and publicise his activities.

So even where there is a partnership between the Mistress and slave in the other world secrecy is the norm. Sometimes if travelling they can go to meetings of other like minded people in another part of the country or abroad and be open about their state, But locally they may want to keep things secret and all their toys hidden away.

For those men whose lives are complicated by having a slave /Mistress relationship outside their "normal" lives things are more extreme. They may have a wife and family at home, and lots of fiends who know nothing of their slave role. For them the slave /Mistress relationship needs to be kept secret and they must learn never to confuse the two. They must be careful to keep the "normal" life normal and the slave life separate.
Emails, texts and phone calls are all risky and must be done using a separate email site and a phone where messages and numbers are routinely cleared daily. They need to look "normal" when they return home in the evening or after a weekend away with Mistress and not to be marked so as they give the game away.

Anything they wear hidden under their clothing needs to remain hidden, which may produce difficulties if it needs washing or cleaning. They need to have a car which looks as normal even if there is a bag of toys in the boot. They must not smell of Mistress's perfume or her cigarettes. All their toys need to be hidden and may need to be kept with Mistress.

They must do all they can to reduce the risk of being found out, and this includes having convincing alibis for where they have been and what they have been doing. If the wife/partner suspects them there are so many ways She can find out. If She finds out and does not understand, or indeed even if She does understand what has been going on, then this can be catastrophic and the end of the marriage or relationship.

All of this leaves the Mistress on Her own and with secrecy essential for her slaves and probably for her also. If She spends Her days flogging slaves then the neighbours may suspect that something is going on from the cries and groans and the frequent visitors. Neighbours may complain if her slaves are seen naked crawling about the garden in full view of next door or even their children.

So being a Mistress is a secret life and being a slave is also mainly a secret life to prevent outside interference and to allow things to continue.

Even with all the care and secrecy needed for a slave who is also in a more traditional relationship the time spent with Mistress under Her control and as Her slave is so good.

If the Mistress and slave can get away for a weekend or even a week away then both of them can live life more in their real roles and state as slave and Mistress and that is even better. But even here toys need to be kept in a closed case so as not to disturb the hotel staff, and the slave may need to take off his collar and chastity to get through airport security though he can always put them on again once this is done and travel with no keys but everything held by Mistress as it should be. This secret life may be difficult but it is still so much better for a man who seeks to be submissive and a slave than bottling it all up inside him and living only half a life.

(See also; contracts, fetish, ownership, safe and sane, safe word, training)

S is for sensory Deprivation

If i am blindfolded i lose my sight and have to depend upon my other senses. This means that sound, touch, smell and taste are all much more sensitive. When Mistress blindfolds me i feel the touch of her hand or her flogger much more than if i can see. But i also do not know what is coming next. The paddle on my backside feels more powerful and i do not know when the blow will fall.

Mistress can shock me, twist my nipples or crush my balls with no warning so a session becomes even more intense.

But sensory deprivation can also be a major part of bondage. i am locked away in a cage or cupboard in chains or zipped into a body bag. i am deprived of sight but ear plugs can take out my hearing too. This means that all i can do is feel the tightness of my bonds and i have no idea of time.

Without sight, cast into darkness and without hearing i just stay there as long as Mistress wants. i drift between waking and sleeping and each time i wake i have no idea of how long i have been here. i just know it is where i should be and Mistress wants it so.

It all leaves me disorientated so i have no idea how long things have been going on. This leaves me vulnerable and shows Mistress holds all the cards.

(See also; bondage, blindfold, darkness and disorientation, isolation, overnight session, sensation and stimulation, paddle)

S is for Sensation and Stimulation

There are so many ways Mistress can stimulate a slave. Her stimuli can be soft and sensuous with the touch of her fingers run along my skin, cool liquid to drink, or her stroking my hair, my face or my nipples.

The stimuli can be harsh with the nails digging into my balls or nipples suddenly and without warning. Her nails can scrape the skin, making patterns before being pushed deep into my skin so it is grabbed and squeezed between the sharpened talons.

When Mistress wants She can come so close that i can smell her exquisite perfume or She can spray me with air freshener so i can smell only that. If i am given food to eat laced with hot chillies it will make my mouth burn and my mouth can be filled with her cigarette ash. The tastes i receive are what She wants.

With the electrics the sensation can be mild like a soft buzzing or vibration or sharp, severe and continuous so i am in agony.

The flogger can be drawn across my back so i feel each strand as it passes which is deeply sensuous, or it can be whacked down hard to force the breath out of my lungs.

When Mistress controls my breathing i breathe when She allows it and i breathe in air warmed by Her mouth.

There are just so many sensations and they overwhelm me. Being a slave at the hands of Mistress, helpless in bondage and controlled by Her leads me into a world of sensory stimulation so intense. But

She decides what it shall be. i can only wait to see what happens next.

Sometimes the combination of sensory deprivation and sensory stimuli become so good that i enter a world where all my senses are so heightened that i am totally overwhelmed. The total effect is so great that all i want is more, more, more until i am left exhausted, worn out and in bliss which lasts for hours or days.

(See also: blindfold, bondage, breath control, electrics, flogging, food control, isolation, nails, sensory deprivation)

S is for sex

For a slave the issue of sex is relatively simple: it is not his to control.

For the slave whose Mistress is a Professional Dominant there is not going to be any sex. A slave may be allowed to kiss Her feet or boots but that is all. They may have agreed a chastity contract and be locked away in a chastity device without access to the key. They will probably have been banned from all masturbation at any time. Mistress is the key holder and has control and there will be NO sex.

Things are a little different for a slave whose partner or wife is his Mistress. There chastity may also be enforced with a locked chastity device. Masturbation may be banned. The slave may not be allowed sex or if he is it is only when Mistress/partner decides it. She is in control. Of course even if Her slave is locked away She can still require stimulation with his mouth to bring her to orgasm as often as She wants. He will be locked up but maybe released from the chastity to serve her when She decides to allow it. He remains in a state of frustrated arousal all the time ready subject to the rules of his key holder, the power of his Mistress. he may be forbidden from even begging for sex, and any begging may increase his time locked away. She decides if She wants him unlocked. She decides. If She wants him unlocked often then this is what will happen.

Slavery is so much about sex and sexual arousal. The things Mistress does to him, the way She dresses. The way She stands and dominates are all sexually exciting. She can touch him wherever and whenever She wants but he is constrained often in bondage. It is all so sexually exciting but he will also probably be in a chastity device so that excitement gives him pain as his penis is crushed within the chastity tube.

If Mistress wants him to be her sex slave he may need training. Most men have little idea of how to use their mouth to bring a woman to orgasm. He may need instruction videos and books to teach him what to do. As a sex slave he is there to serve Mistress. Whether he is ever allowed to get his penis out of its chastity device depends on Mistress alone.

For me masturbation is banned and i wear a chastity device during the day when out of the house. Sex is only permitted when my partner wishes it, and it is always in the position of Her choice. i am controlled from without and spend my wife aroused and frustrated but it is so good and a major part for me of being a slave. i am content but in reality i have chosen this path and my choices are no longer my own but are made for me.

(See also; chastity, chastity contract, contracts, masturbation, personal services, training, strap on)

S is for Shock collar

A shock collar is an electronic device used on dogs to control them. The dog wears the device around its neck. A signal from the remote controller leads to an electrical discharge into the dog's neck which is unpleasant. Alternatively the collar can be programmed to activate if the dog goes near a boundary fence protected by a wire to signal to the shock collar to prevent the dog from leaving the space.

In humans placing such a collar around the neck is dangerous with the electrical discharge giving a risk of cardiac irregularities. But it can be fitted around a thigh or wrapped around the balls so that when the Mistress presses the control button the slave gets a shock. This can be mild as a warning or severe

It can be used as a call system for a slave to drop anything he is doing and attend Mistress. It can be used to punish a slave with severe shocks that bring him to his knees and crying out with the pain. It is good for use out of doors to summon or to use at Mistress's whim.

In a restaurant the slave has no idea of when he may be shocked or how severely and must sit still. If a group of Mistress's friends are present the controller can be passed around and the slave have no idea of who may shock him next. It allows the slave to know he is controlled, and can with some systems be used to remotely control him up to 400 yards away or even further. Mistress enjoys using it when we are out and it shows Her power over me. She loves to place the controller on the table in front of Her to remind me then shock if i move or just for fun.

(See also: electrics, violet wand, zapped)

S is for Shopping

Mistress has need for fresh candles, groceries and all sorts of things. A slave can be expected to attend with all of these for his Mistress or sent out, often in some form of bondage under his clothes
to get things for Mistress. he must get exactly what She wants, the correct brand, the correct size; anything else is failure and will be punished.

If the slave is attending Mistress he is there to serve. he is there to attend Her when shopping, opening doors, stand quietly when She is looking at things, pay for what Mistress wants, and carry Her bags. he may be controlled with the shock collar and be in bondage under his clothes.

Between shops he may have his lead grasped firmly by Mistress to keep him under control all the time.

Many Mistresses enjoy shopping and having a slave to act as their driver, porter, and door opener is good. he is the person to carry an umbrella to make sure She is dry even if he is getting wet. he may be expected to wear her uniform when he does this. he can be left outside a shop or in a corner for hours whilst She decides what to buy , if anything. he is there to serve Her needs totally.

On occasions Mistress may want to spend a whole day shopping going from shop to shop. A slave should remember that his place is to serve no matter how long this may be and keep quiet never complaining. Anything less is cause for severe punishment even in public where he may deserve a slap or a severe shock to bring him to his knees.

Mistress and slave may want new toys or bondage gear to try. he should fund it but She will buy on line and he will not know what She has new to use to torment or punish him or hold him in bondage until it arrives.

Mistress takes shopping seriously and so also must Her slave in serving Her.
(See also: bondage, domestic service, fetish, leash, ownership, power)

S is for Sissy

At school a sissy was a child who tended to cry if he fell over or was bullied. In adult men it is a term of abuse applied to those who do not show the manly virtues. It also applies to those who dress in women's clothes often at the requirement of a Mistress who does so to humiliate them.

A man who has been made into a sissy is expected to take on what are often seen as "feminine roles". he may be required to dress in female clothes and have his male underwear disposed of so he must always wear female pants or even a bra.

He may be expected to wear an apron and even a "French Maid" uniform when he does the cleaning, cooking etc. he is expected to take over all the household tasks to clean and cook and tidy, to wash and iron and put away. he will be expected to defer to any woman as his superior in any situation and never to stand up for himself. he must be submissive to all at all times.

This is all so different from the stereotype of male appearance and behaviour and adds to the humiliation and degradation of the male slave.

Sissification is the process by which this progresses step by step until he is totally changed into the appearance and behaviour his Mistress desires.

(See also: Brazilian wax, domination, forced feminization, humiliation)

S is for Sound

Mistress may have favourite sounds, tracks, songs and music that She enjoys. She may want to use these as the background when She flogs and beats Her slaves. The rhythm and pattern She chooses may get Her into rhythm for the flogging.

She may want a background of music or rhythm so that neighbours are not disturbed by the sound of beating or the cries of the beaten slave.

Sound can also be used to manipulate slaves. If he is blindfolded and bound and She plays heavy hard rhythms She may disorientate him. White noise which is a hissing sound like an out of tune radio makes it difficult for him to think and if played at high volume can even be painful.

When a Mistress uses sound as the background to her tormenting a slave he begins to associate the sounds with what is done to him. If this is done repeatedly he will know to expect particular torment if he hears the music and prepare himself.

Mistress may also have particular music or tracks She wants to listen to when She is having her feet or shoulders massaged. She may want relaxing music for her bath. Slaves must learn what Mistress wants and make sure it is available to her. This includes keeping an eye on her favourite singers and bands and getting downloads for her or CDs when they come out.

But Mistress has her favourites She likes to play and that is the music that the slaves must get used to. Not what he likes in the car when he is driving Her on a shopping trip but what She wants must be available and this is what matters.

Mistress has Her taste in music and Her taste rules.

(See also: flogging, isolation, sensation and stimulation, sensory deprivation)

S is for Spanking

Children are spanked on the bottom when they are naughty in some societies but spanking in adults is much more about sexual excitement and stimulation.

When a slave is spanked he may be bent forward or draped across the knees of the person who is doing the spanking. The hand comes down on the bottom with a slapping sound. Repeated blows warm up the backside turning it a pink then a red colour. Often the blows are interspersed with rubbing the skin. All this stimulation is very arousing especially if the private parts are compressed against the thighs of the person doing the spanking. Blow follows blow and the whole backside begins to feel so hot. For a slave in chastity it gets difficult as he begins to get an erection but it is prevented by the device.

Spanking is such good fun, and many people who are not into BDSM or slavery use spanking as a part of foreplay. Slaves can be spanked at any time but it can also be to warm them up for a more severe beating with paddle, flogger, can or whip. There are groups that are all into spanking where they meet for lots and lots of spanking and where a slave can be passed around and spanked by different people again and again and again through a whole evening.

One advantage of spanking is that it requires no equipment. The only issue is whether the person being spanked consents and whether the sound might disturb others in neighbouring rooms.

It does not require the slave to be naked or undressed. All they need to do is to slip down their pants to expose the buttocks. If desired the person to be spanked can be spanked fully dressed though much of the excitement and intensity comes from the direct skin to skin contact.

Spanking can be hard work for the Mistress. It may make her hand smart and repeated spanking work can lead to a build up of hard skin on the palm of her hand. This is why some Mistresses prefer to use a glove for spanking to protect their skin. But if the glove is rough or studded then the person spanked is going to find it so much more painful.

Spanking is the simplest form of impact play, but it can be combined with the use of all other implements, paddles, tawse, floggers, canes and whips. After a slave has been paddled or caned even a mild spanking on such a tender backside feels severe. Heavy spanking can leave the backside swollen, red and bruised and it feels tender for days whenever the slave sits down. he is reminded of the spanking on sitting and may prefer to stand to reduce the discomfort. Now is the time he may be required to sit on a hard seat or even a mat with bristles if the Mistress wants to make things more difficult for him.

i love to be spanked by Mistress and being passed around at a spanking party by Mistress for others to spank was so exciting and also quite painful. But not as much as when Mistress spanks me Herself.

(See also: crop, cane, paddle, flogging, tawse, whip, punishment)

S is for Spanx

Spanx is the trademark of a clothing company who make clothing with a large quantity of elastane in it. It compresses the person inside and is used for compression stockings, pants, body shaping garments and to help a woman get the appearance She chooses.

It crushes the person inside just like a corset. Spanx pants are so tight that they feel as if everything inside is being crushed including the cock and balls. If there are high pants the top tends to roll down and form a tight band so it feels as if there is an iron band around the tummy.

Being dressed in spanx from top to toe with vest, pants, and tights presses in from every side and makes exercise difficult. The person wearing it is crushed like with a corset but it is all over from neck to toes. This feels good but it is difficult if it is worn under clothes for travelling or for work. But being made to wear spanx under clothes shows Mistress control of all of a slave's body.

Hoods can be made of the same material but with an air hole for breathing . Elastane is also used in "Darlex" where there are two layers of elastane with a rubberised layer between them. This is used for tight hoods and body bags and once zipped inside the slave is helpless. he may try to move but the material prevents him. he can try to struggle but it is in vain. Elastanc in clothing changes the silhouette and is body shaping so it can be used to crush a slave and imprison him and make him look as Mistress requires; slim, and tight all produced by something hidden under his outside clothes.

(See also: corsets and compressive clothing, forced feminization, fetish, humiliation)

S is for Spreader bar

If Mistress wants my ankles or wrists held together She can link my cuffs with a lock or a short chain. Alternatively She can use a rigid bar with one wrist or ankle or each end.

If the wrist cuffs are held wide apart the slave cannot do anything which requires the hands put together and has no possibility of getting out of the cuffs. The bar can also be used to suspend him on tiptoe by his arms.

A spreader bar between the ankles allows the legs to be kept well apart. No way for the slave to put their legs together to protect their private parts. The bar can also be pulled up to lift up the feet for a bastinado session of beating on the soles of the feet or even higher so the slave is suspended upside down.

If the bar is short it acts as a hobble and makes it difficult for the slave to walk. However Mistress decides to secure he slave She knows what She wants to do with him.

(See also: cuffs, chains, bondage, suspension)

S is for Straightjacket

In Psychiatric hospitals inmates were placed in a straightjacket to prevent them harming themselves. It is a jacket which has arms ending in mittens with no fingers. The jacket is put on from the front and secured with straps at the back out of reach. There are also straps which fit under the groins to prevent it riding up and coming off.

Once the person is in the jacket the arms are wrapped around the body and secured with straps or chains which are built in to the arms. The individual has no further use of his arms and cannot get free.

Straightjackets can be made of heavy canvas, leather or rubber. They allow a slave to be secured but still able to use his legs. This allows him to be moved around and a straightjacket covered by a coat will allow a slave to be transported by car. he can be walked to the car and strapped in, and the straightjacket is covered by his coat. Nothing is visible to the outside observer.

Because the straightjacket is inescapable it can be combined with other bondage for long periods of restraint with the slave hooded and with ankles secured as well. A slave in a straightjacket is not going to be able to escape so it works well for overnight bondage, whether or not the slave is also locked in a cupboard, a cage or even a strong wooden box.

The main advantage over the use of a body bag is that the slave still has the use of his legs and can move around though his trunk is enclosed and his hands wrapped around his body. Some straightjackets have flaps covering the nipple areas which can be removed and most do not cover the genitalia or backside so these are all available to Mistress to use when tormenting him

(See also: bondage, bondage bag, cage, cupboard, isolation, kidnapping, overnight sessions)

S is for Strap on

A strap on harness fits around the waist with straps between the thighs to the back. This provides the anchorage for a dildo shaped like a penis or in any other shape. If a Mistress wears this She appears to have a penis sticking out rigid before Her.

The sight is intimidating to most slaves. Their penis and balls are locked away in chastity and can do nothing. Mistress now has a penis which She can use on them.

She may make them kneel before her and suck "Her Cock" for as long as She likes. It may be forced to the back of their mouth and held there filling their mouth as a gag whilst She flogs them or twists their nipples. The slave is humiliated, and shown that he is no longer a man but just a plaything of Mistress.

She may use the strap on dildo to force entrance into his anus fucking him from behind and using him. He feels the size of the dildo entering him and the movements in and out as Mistress moves around. The slave is now totally in the power of Mistress as She shows her power over him and his place as one who can be fucked when and if She desires it.

He has agreed all of this but it still comes as a shock. He really is now less than a man as he is used by his Mistress. he may never have had any male/male sex in his life, and have no desire to be penetrated by a man, but Mistress has the power and the strap on to do it to him anyway.

The strap on is an implement that Mistresses can use if they want to humiliate their slaves and to teach them their true position as an

inferior to the High and Superior Mistress. The strap on teaches the slave his position in life. he is vulnerable, submitting to Mistress, and accepting Her dildo inside him because She wants it.
It really shows Her power over him.

he may also find he likes it as well.

(See also: dildo, domination, humiliation, ownership, masturbation, sex)

S is for Stocks

Stocks were used for securing people for public humiliation and to allow the public to throw things at them. The convicted person was secured bending forward with their hands and neck fixed between two blocks of wood set on top of a post so they could not get away or use their arms to protect themselves. Then the crowd would pelt them with things, including rotting food and they would have to stay there for as long as their sentence stated.

With a slave the stocks are similar. He is secured bending forward with head and hands secured between the two blocks of wood or steel frame which have cut out holes to allow the neck and wrists to be secured. Once helpless he can be pelted with things, or flogged, spanked or beaten on the back or backside or have things pushed inside him. As he stands there bending forward he is well placed for weights to be hung on his nipples or his balls and he will find the position uncomfortable the longer he is kept there.

These can be made by a slave for his Mistress or bought from commercial suppliers. Some stocks have places to secure the ankles as well as the wrists and one type uses two planks of wood with cut outs to hold the wrists and ankles so the slave is forced to lean forward in a position which is rapidly very uncomfortable.

Most couples will not have access to stocks unless they build them themselves but many commercial dungeon chambers have these available so they are often used by Professional Dominants on their clients and in those chambers which can be hired for a period by a Mistress and Her slave they are something worth trying.

i made a set of stocks for Mistress which allow her either to place my neck and wrists in them or both wrists and ankles. They are padded to prevent chafing but it is difficult to be in them for long without becoming uncomfortable. This does not count discomfort provided by anything else that Mistress wishes to do to me whilst i am locked in the stocks.

(See also: cage, cupboard, dungeon, bondage, paddles, flogging, whip)

S is for Submission

Submission is the key to open the door into a life of pleasure for a man who seeks to explore this side of his life. If he is exploring the world of BDSM and starts to attend professional Dominant Mistresses he will discover that this gives him an opportunity to begin to see how good it can be to submit to another.

Even if it starts just in short sessions where he hands over control of himself to a Mistress it will grow as he discovers that it feels good to submit. So many men live lives where they are expected to be the one in control. They work and continuously have to make decisions. When they get home they may be the person who makes the decisions there as well. But inside they want to let go and be under the control of another.

Once a man starts down the road of slavery giving control to a Mistress She can help him to expand this into many areas of his life. He does not just have the opportunity to submit for an hour or two. He can be helped so it is 24/7 even if he is not under direct control but controlled from afar.

If a man seeks to be put under control then chastity is a good place to start. He voluntarily gives up control over his orgasms and the ability to masturbate and wears a chastity device which controls him. Mistress is the key holder and he has lost control of this essential part of his life. Even if he can only wear the chastity device part of the time he can be held to chastity the rest of the time and banned from masturbation. If he fails he must inform his Mistress and take the consequences.

Domestic and personal services for Mistress allow him the opportunity to serve. he submits himself as Her servant. Her needs come first. He must do what She wants and fulfil her needs and desires. This gives him so many things he can do for Her. Even if he does not like cleaning or any other task She sets him it does not matter. he is having the opportunity to submit and to serve and that is rewarding even on its own.

he will be given the chance to show his submission by wearing a collar which shows that he is Her slave. She may want him to wear ankle or wrist chains to remind him as well. She may want him to wear female pants or tights, a corset and spanx under his clothes which give him the opportunity to submit still further. Each step he takes down this road reinforces his submission and builds his submissive nature still further.

When he is with Mistress She will allow him to submit his body to Her control. She will place him in bondage and once bound he is helpless and his submission becomes more difficult to reverse. Even if he has a safe word he will not want to use it. he agrees that She has control over his penis and balls and can lock them away. She controls his arse and can beat it, cane it and push things into it. His nipples belong to Her and She can enjoy herself playing with them. She will decide when he is in bondage and of what type and how She wants to play with Her slave. She decides on how and when to chastise him and what implement She will use.

When he is with Mistress he submits himself to Her. She decides on whether he can talk or be kept silent. She decides to use a blindfold or to have him hooded. She decides if She wants to fuck him with the strap on.

As a slave a man has the opportunity to discover the freedom of submission so that all parts of him the whole body and more important the whole mind are both taken into the control of his Mistress.

None of this will happen overnight. He cannot go from no submission to total submission and keep to it in a short while. It may take years for the relationship of a slave and His Mistress to blossom and grow that he can submit wholeheartedly and feel the freedom that comes from submission.

Many men discover that they like to submit at an early age but it takes them years to begin to do it. If your Mistress is your partner then submission can take a whole extra dimension. Women are superior by nature and this is true. A man who wishes to understand this needs to realise that submission to the Woman is natural and makes things better. It all depends on whether a partner wishes his submission or not. he can offer it in little things. he can start by listening to her and discovering what She wants and then accepting it and not having a row when he want to do something else. This is not BDSM but common senses and reduces tension and allows for more fun and pleasure in most relationships. It does not have to be explicit with him agreeing to be her slave but just acting as if Her needs are so important to him that he wants to follow them.

If he truly wishes to learn to submit then She may be prepared to begin to live is a more assertive way and he can help Her. They can have a female lead relationship where Her word is final even if it appears not to be the case. She can be given the chance to control sex as She wants it. he will need to learn her needs and desires and to provide for them. Many women seek intimacy and sharing more than just sex and more men want more sex than intimacy. So a man exploring his submissive side can take effort to find out what intimacy means to his partner and to listen, to share, and to do the things that improve it. Simple things like always taking out the trash or buying flowers regularly or keeping all his stuff tidy and not in the way will help. Offering to take over part of the house work or shopping to give her time is useful.Making it clear that he does not want to be off on "men's nights out or weekends away with his friends shows She is in control. None of this has any outward appearance of "submission or slavery" but it will enhance Her life and makes things better. If She wants things can go further and She can take formal control of sex, get him to do the majority of the housework, control his free time and the family money and have the deciding word on plans for holidays new jobs, and the direction of travel in life for both of them. Here She is truly in control and he will be living a life of submission to Her will. Few women may want to go that far, but giving up control of the television remote control to a partner and not arranging time out without her agreement are easy to consider though not always easy to do.

i have found that the urge to submit grows in me every year. i started by exploring bondage with Professional Dominants for short sessions and this has changed over the years until now i live three lives at the same time. There is my life at work where i have control over some things and have to submit to superiors as well. i used to find this difficult and get angry if ordered to do something i thought was stupid or unlikely to succeed.   Now i will still argue my case and push hard for what i think is right but if the decision goes against me then i am less bothered and less "personally" involved.

It makes me more relaxed and it is easier to get on at work and has helped my career as well. This surprised me as i feared that not always showing the total confidence at work would work against me but now i am seen as more of a team player and able to be flexible. So learning to submit when necessary at work has come from submission in the rest of my life.

At home i have a partner who is not into female leadership and was not interested when i broached the subject of wishing to submit to Her in the past on several occasions. But She likes the attention i give her. She likes the control of sex and the television remote control and She likes it that i spoil her and do my share around the home more. She likes to have "Her "bed prepared for her at night, the house tidy and Her breakfast place ready for when She gets up. She likes the freedom to decide where to go on holiday and the fact there are less rows as i always give in and submit to her plans for my diet, my haircut and my clothing and do not fight back as i used to. There may be no formal female lead relationship but She is certainly the leader now at home and this gives me great pleasure.

But i am also a slave and property of my Mistress. She controls me and i am allowed to attend Her and serve Her. She is training me in submission and i really did need a trainer. With Her there is no limit to Her power and my submission and it is this that spills over into other areas of my life. It took me years to get here and there is still far to go but for me submission to a Mistress and to women in general now seems the way to go for me. i find such deep content in submitting now to Mistress that it is always a pleasure no matter what She may want. i may spend part of my time in the chains and collar that signify my slavery but inside the chains are there permanently and my slavery has become internalised and a major part of who i am

(See also: chains, chastity, collars, female supremacy, female lead relationships, ownership, sex, training)

S is for Stress positions

In the interrogation of suspects stress positions are used to put the subject into a situation where he is stressed and more likely to give information or confess to a crime. In most societies this is not legal for the police or judicial authorities but it has certainly been used by the military in war situations and from time to time has got well out of hand. It is not quite torture but it is close to it and in some countries the two go hand in hand.

Of course there are problems in that a subject who has been tortured will say anything to get out of the torture so information gained this way is rarely reliable.

Mistresses use stress positions in bondage on their slaves to make things more intense. If the slave is comfortable in bondage and is left he may well just drift off to sleep. But if he is made to stand on tiptoes or kneeling head to the floor or bound so that the can neither lift his head or straighten his legs then this is a stress position and the bondage is more severe. If he is shouted at by Mistress or She spits in his face, or She keeps him in the dark or plays loud music to disorientate him She is increasing the intensity of the experience.

So stress positions can be used to enhance bondage. They include kneeling head to the floor, sitting cross legged with collar attached to ankles, the stocks or rack, making him stand on one leg or on tip toes with the position made more difficult with a rope around the balls that will tighten if he comes off his toes, any position that keeps him bent or stretched or kept so he cannot more will become stressful over time and this is made greater if he is sitting on a backside that has been recently spanked or caned.
Hooding him increases the tension and using heat and cold enhance it further. Sitting a slave on aboard covered in spikes or upturned beer bottle tops makes the act of sitting stressful.

(See also: bondage, hoods, chains, predicament bondage, torment and torture)

S is for Suspension

A slave who is suspended hangs free, twisting in his bonds and totally helpless. he is totally controlled by the bondage and cannot even touch the floor. He may be hanging in and harness upright or upside down or rotated at Mistress's pleasure. It is a wonderful idea and there are lots and lots of images of slaves in bondage suspended in all sorts of positions often in rope bondage and providing a very artistic appearance.

However it is not as easy as it seems and there are lots of dangers. Many of the images are taken on people secured by experts and only kept in that position for a few moments to take their photograph and are not suitable as examples of suspension bondage. It can only be done if both the person doing the suspension and the person suspended understand the risks and have agreed them. Even then a quick way of getting the slave out of the suspension safely may be needed especially if he begins to feel unwell. The suspension point needs to be secure. If you are considering suspension at home, and having a slave suspended over the stairs then you need a secure point for the suspension which will take at least three times the weight of a slave. In general it needs to take 240Kg or more weight without breaking free, and the ropes or suspension wires involved need to be able to take an equivalent strain. Otherwise things may break and the slave fall to the floor or even further down the stairs with the risk of breaking limbs, ribs, severe head injury or even a broken neck or back.

On the whole this is not something for the inexperienced and training is necessary including safety training. Many commercial dungeons have suspension apparatus and the owner will keep it well maintained and show how it is used. Simple suspension in a strap cage or a cage is possible where the slave is enclosed in a bag or cage and that is elevated off the floor.

If the suspension is upright then a body harness is needed as if the suspension is by the shoulders alone then they may be dislocated with the weight of the body. If there is upside down suspension by the ankles then the ankle straps need to be robust and designed for the purpose with strong links none of which can break. Many dungeons have suspension controlled by an electric controller with a wire up to a winch on the ceiling and a 1000 kg breaking strain wire with a hook at the end.

A slave suspended upright can feel claustrophobic if in a bag and need to be let out. if they are kept upright for any time there is a risk of fainting and if kept upright when fainting then convulsions can occur or even death. If a slave is upside down then he may quickly black out and need to be lowered to the ground. If part of the body harness is rope bondage this can tighten around the body, crush and tear the skin or tighten so that there is difficulty breathing or compression of the circulation or on nerves to cause damage. So suspension is not to be undertaken lightly or the person in suspension left alone. But it does feel great and looks good too.

(See also bondage, chain, safe and sane)

S is for Switch

If you take a flexible branch from a tree, strip off the bark and make sure it is cleaned you have a switch. This can be used to beat slaves a little like using a cane. Because the branch is flexible it will work well to sting his backside. If the surface of the switch is rough or the bark is left on then the impact becomes much more powerful. The roughness can mean there is a risk of tearing the skin, bruising and bleeding. So a switch might seem milder than a cane but can be more severe.

All sorts of branches can be used. If a willow species is used then it will be very flexible. The thicker the branch the more rigid it becomes so a branch thicker than the dimensions of a little finger will be like using a plank of wood. If a bunch of birch branches is used this can provide a very serious device for thrashing slaves. In Singapore and some other places they still use the cane for punishing criminals. In the Isle of Man until recently bunches of birch rods were used on those guilty of minor offences. In the Roman Republic and Empire magistrates had carried before them the bunch of rods "the Fasces" used to beat people as a sign of their authority. The fascists of Italy in the 20th century used the same symbol and name for themselves.

So just because you have taken a flexible branch to beat your slave it can still be severe, especially if it still has thorns on it when the area beaten will be shredded ad torn.

Another use of the word switch is in describing those who occasionally take the submissive role and sometimes the dominant position. They may describe themselves as a switch. They may be predominantly dominant but like to be flogged or put in bondage from time to time, It could be they are predominantly submissive but permitted to act in a dominant manner by their Mistress with another slave.

For me Mistress is supreme and i am Her slave and Her property. i agree with ideas of Female Supremacy and want to be in a Female Lead Relationship and life. i cannot see myself ever acting as a switch and dominating a woman and equally i find that submission and obedience to women is right for me.

For me i see no possibility of being a switch but i know others who do switch from time to time.

(See also: cane, domination, flogging, submission, whips)

T is for Tattoo

A tattoo is for life so for a slave to get tattooed with a logo for Mistress, Her name or some mark to designate him as a slave is a big step.

But it can be small and not conspicuous. It could be between the cheeks of his buttocks where it will not be seen or be a series of initials or a flower motif to signify to Mistress and slave what is going on though innocuous in itself. A tattoo of the slave's bar code of his slave registration number will only show he is a slave to those who know of such things.

There are always risks to tattooing so it needs to be done by a trained tattooist with fresh and sterile needles, cleanliness and all steps to reduce the risk of infection. Even here infection is still a risk particularly if the area to be tattooed such as the buttock cleft might be damp.

A slave who is going to be tattooed needs to remember that anyone who sees his body will see it so if he has a partner who is against tattoos and he comes home with a tattoo of flower on his backside or thigh She will wonder what is going on.

i yearn for a tattoo to show i belong to Mistress but cannot have one for that reason. Unfortunately the same applies to a brand as well. But there are always temporary tattoos to wear when i am away with Mistress which proclaim me "Slave" and remind her to "Use me". They stay on for several days and need to be scrubbed off. It is a little like Her painting my toe nails with nail varnish to show She owns my feet.

(See also: ownership, branding)

T is for Tawse

In English schools, before it was made illegal, corporal punishment tended to be with the sole of a slipper or the cane. In Scotland the tawse was used instead.

A tawse is a leather strap, usually split at the end into two tails which can be used for beating a slave. Mistress can use a leather belt instead often doubled with the buckle end held in her hand and the loop of leather striking the slave. Most tawses are made of leather of the same type of leather as the belt but it is possible to get ones made of heavy rubber, occasionally split to give three tails not two.

The blow delivered by a tawse sounds loud and stings, especially the where the tails hit. Given with full force it is very powerful and can bruise or cut the skin.

It is difficult to know if the pain from a wooden paddle or a tawse is more severe. As the blindfolded slave does not know which implement Mistress will be using he may find out when She uses both on his backside.

(See also: crop, cane, flogging, paddle, spanking, whip)

T is for Temperment

There is a wide range of temperments among those who are into dominance and submission. Some are totally dominant, some switch from one to the other and many like me are totally submissive.

But even here some are more submissive than others. Those attending a Professional Dominant for the occasional session may only wish to submit for short periods. Others seek the life of slavery or become the property of their Mistress. his submission is a given and the slave needs now to train himself and to be trained by his Mistress to allow him to be a slave all the time.

Mistress needs a slave who will always obey her and always remember his place in Her service. The slave may have a submissive temperment but he will still need training so he never forgets this if this is to be 24/7.

Regular training helps him develop and his underlying temperment to show.

But even with submissives there are varieties of response to pain. Some Mistresses really like to give pain to their slaves and show a sadistic streak. They really enjoy inflicting the pain.

Some slaves are happy to be flogged and beaten and sense that Mistress likes it and enjoys it and so they learn to like it too. Others see their ability to withstand pain as important to them in some "macho" kind of way. But there are those slaves who really like the pain. They enjoy the beating and the pain that Mistress delivers. Some will even disobey mistress for the opportunity to be punished. Most slaves accept punishment as what they must suffer if they fail but do their best not to fail as they do not like to be punished.

But there are those who truly enjoy the pain and consider themselves "masochists" and see that the pain arouses them and gives them more enjoyment than anything else.

Most of us slaves are a mixture of dominant and submissive but tending to the submissive which is why we become slaves in the first case. At the same time some see themselves as service orientated and seek to serve Mistress and others and others are more of a "pain slut". But whatever the temperament it is Mistress who is in control and a slave will get what She wants him to have.

(See also: fetish, domination, punishment, submission, switch)

T is for Time

It takes time to set up some forms of bondage, especially rope bondage or complex suspension so there is little point doing it if the time for a session is going to be short.

Burt short sessions can be good and so intense with so much happening that the slave is overwhelmed by the bondage, the beating, and all that happens.

Long sessions of several hours allow so much more to be done. There is time to put the slave "down" in a bag, cage or cupboard or to arrange bondage satisfying to both Mistress and slave and which looks artistically satisfying as well. There is time for a leisurely long session of flogging, caning and paddling with no risk of running out of time.

But best of all are very long sessions of 24 hours, a weekend or even a week. This gives the slave time to live life fully as a slave, to serve and to keep to his slave state the whole time. he can forget about time and live totally in the moment. Of course if he is disorientated as to whether it is day or night from long periods hooded or in sensory deprivation he will have no idea of time at all.

In an ideal world i would be slave to Mistress 24/7 under her control night and day for the rest of my life. This would allow her to mould and train me to serve her as She wants and to do so all the time.

But even when that is not possible there are ways to increase the time i spend as a slave. i have training to do, cat food and water for lunch, exercise regimes every evening, and i live in a chastity device all day and a butt plug at night. When i am out of the house i am in ankle chains and collar and often nipple clamps and special clothing as well. i am reminded that i am a slave all the time,. i am able to give time to Mistress writing these reports and blogs for her. Every day there is something to do.

So for me it is 24/7 slavery, just not always possible to express it openly in my life but when i am with Mistress it is the real thing and there is never enough time as i always want to be more in Her presence and serving Her. Then time is the enemy but we make the best use of it that we can.

(See also: contracts, ownership, training)

T is for tights

Tights are worn by women to cover and adorn their legs. Some are thin and almost transparent whilst others are patterned and may be thicker. Some tights have elastane or lycra as part of their material and tend to be more stretchy and tight. They can be used to compress the legs and prevent swelling and the development of clots when on long journeys or to prevent blood pooling in the legs leading to fainting.

Those tights with lots of elastic material in them can be extremely tight indeed and act to shape the appearance of the body. Combined with thick elasticated pants, top or corselet they can tighten up the appearance of the legs, buttocks or tummy to give a thinner appearance.

Some women like to wear stockings which either hold up or are held up by a garter belt and garters and these can look very sexy.

But for the male slave the wearing of tights is because Mistress wants it. She wants him to feel that She is making him dress like a woman under his clothing, and may combine this with forcing him to throw away his male boxer shorts and wear coloured women's briefs or a thong. This is to sissify him, to reduce his apparent manhood and to humiliate him. It may be a part of deliberate forced (though agreed by the slave) feminization.

Another reason why a slave may be required to live in tights is that they are so very tight. He is crushed from the waist down or even all over by tight constrictive clothing. He may be forced to wear a vest with a corset beneath it and tights just extend that crushing all the way to his toes. Here it is control that the Mistress is seeking over Her slave and once encased in tights at least one size too small and designed to shape the body and legs he is crushed indeed and will not forget that this is on the orders of Mistress

i reported to Mistress that when i had worn anti-embolism stockings for a long flight to prevent clots forming i had found them difficult to wear and very tight. Her response was to put me into tight control tights and spanx and i have been crushed daily when i go out ever since. No one can see that i am wearing them under my clothing, but they crush me and have worked well to keep me warm during the winter as a side effect. Wearing them i can never forget that Mistress has ordered them and to regret that i mentioned the anti-embolism stockings in the first place.

(See also: corsets and compressive clothing, forced feminization, sissification)

T is for training

Most men who aspire to be slaves need lots of training. They do not know how to address a Mistress, how to present themselves to Her or what to do. They are lost in their own fantasies and need to be introduced to the reality of being a slave and trained to deliver what She wants.

They have little experience of bondage and a small experience of being flogged or beaten. They may get so excited at the beginning of a session of all they want to do but not be able to cope. So they need training in all areas of being a slave.

i am extremely lucky that i have now been a slave for over 10 years and that all three of the Mistresses i have served in that time have been excellent trainers. i learned early on that a regular relationship with a single Mistress means that they know me and what i can take and i begin to discover their likes and dislikes. They have then been able to take me in hand and develop me both in my descent into submission and slavery and in so many particular areas.

In bondage i have been trained to cope with difficult positions and expect to be kept in bondage for long periods. i have been trained to spend time in cages , cupboards and bondage bags and to cope with periods of sensory deprivation. Initially even a few minutes in a heavy hood made me claustrophobic but now i can cope for several hours.

When i started i had tiny nipples but hours every day wearing nipple training clips means that they have grown so that they can now take larger and more serious gate clamps worn for 12 hours or longer. There is more of a nipple for the Mistress to play with.

Initially i could not cope with the idea of anything being done to my back passage but now Mistress can make me insert butt plugs and dildos or use a strap on on me. Now i spend every night with a butt plug up inside me and am being trained to take larger and larger ones as well.

When i started there was no limitation on my sexual activities and i could masturbate whenever i liked. Now i have been placed in a chastity contract and required to wear a heavy steel chastity device all day every day and 24/7 whenever possible.

When i started i was interested in bondage but did not consider that corporal punishment was something i might like. Mistresses who enjoy CP have trained me to take more and more, and now i find that as they enjoy giving it and flogging me so i enjoy being flogged more and more.

Mistress requires not just obedience from her slaves but also service. i have been taken for training to learn to give Her massage and recently been shown how to put on nail varnish on the toes, used myself as the subject. i have been made to learn about cleaning and all sorts of domestic service and if my performance in this is deficient i have been severely beaten because of my failures. Mistress wants a slave trained to deliver both personal care and domestic service and this has been fun to learn.

What is most amazing is that Mistress has trained me to write these reports and blogs and has got me writing reports, letters for Her and now an A to Z of the life of a male slave. This keeps on bringing up new things for Her to try and so now i write this in tight elastic tights and pants and have been introduced to the pleasure and horror of a tight lacing corset and to be Her ashtray.

Performance always improves with practice and so training is essential for slaves. For me the big thing has been that training by Mistress has shown me that this is the way i want to be and has changed me from someone who liked to spend short periods submitting to a powerful Mistress to one who has been a slave for over 10 years and the property of Mistress for nearly two years. The training has changed me so now this is what i want to be all the time.

So training means effort and training by a Mistress increases Her control over the slave. It develops in him those habits that Mistress wants to see and makes him a better slave. Training lies at the root of how to take things forward in every area of BDSM.

i am just so lucky to have passed through the hands of two excellent trainers who developed me and my present Mistress whose training now takes over so many areas of my life. She has really changed me not for the worse but for the better as I now begin to understand the totally superior position of all Women, seek to live a Female Lead life and to learn how to serve Her better.

A Mistress who is a good trainer understands Her slaves, their possibilities and their limitations and can train them to be better slaves and better people as well, behaving in a better manner, taking notice of what is said to them and capable of domestic ad personal service.   Recently i have been expected to have a regular Brazilian wax as part of my preparation to attend Mistress. i would never have thought of this but it is what Mistress wants and what Mistress wants She MUST get from her slaves.

(See also; bondage, bondage at work, chastity, chastity contracts, contracts, corsets, domination, domestic service ,ownership personal service ,punishment, submission)

T is for trampling

Slaves should be prepared to kneel and prostrate at the feet of their Mistress. This is their proper place.

Once a slave is lying on the floor at the feet of his Mistress She may want to show him that he is no more than a worm to be squashed into the dust. She can do this by pressing down upon him with all Her weight using Her arms or She can sit on him to crush him into the dirt.

Some slaves like to be pressed down by the feet of their Mistress who can walk all over them to trample them. There are risks if She uses too much force and She must be careful not to damage the neck or the back. But She can stand on him with one foot on the back of his neck so he is truly under Her heel, or with one leg and a lot of weight anywhere on his upper back or pelvis. If She is going to walk up and down over him he will need to consent in advance and there is a risk of damage if his bones are weak and Her weight is large.

Even if her weight is small it may be best to start trampling with bare feet to spread the load rather than to be wearing stiletto heels which may puncture the skin or even deeper down into the body.

But to be walked over by one's Mistress really shows a slave his position in life.

Most trampling is carried out indoors in a room with a smooth floor but there is no reason why it cannot be out of doors as well. If

Mistress is out walking with a slave then She does not want Her feet and shoes or boots to be made dirty by a puddle or a patch of mud. The slave can provide the bridge so Her boots stay clean. If there is a patch of nettles she does not want to get stung so the slave can be made to lie down on them, take the stings and protect his Mistress from the nettles as She walks over him

(See also: boots, domination, fetish, ownership),

T is for travel

Slaves typically come to see their Mistress where She is based, but there is no reason why both slave and Mistress cannot travel to new places. If the slave and Mistress are able to travel together or meet in other places they can find time to explore options that may not always be possible at the base Mistress usually uses. If they are able to get away for a night there are dungeons for hire in most countries which are fully equipped. The Mistress and slave can book for an hour or two to play with the equipment, or arrange an overnight stay to give more time for fun. The commercial dungeon will often have a bedroom where the Mistress can sleep comfortably and cages in which the slave can stay overnight. Some dungeons have suspension equipment so this can be tried with a good set of equipment including a powered winch to lift the slave without the need to spend money on it at home.

One other advantage of the slave spending time away with his Mistress is that it gives them more time together to work on developing him as a slave. he can be kept in bondage longer including overnight. he can be expected to serve and provide personal services and make tea and coffee and get drinks. he can be outside with Mistress in a place far from home where neither will be recognised so that simple actions like walking the slave on a lead may be possible.

If Mistress and slave are in a city away from their usual haunts it may be possible to attend fetish or BDSM events which they might not be able to do normally. It is possible also to take advantage of being away to take lessons on rope bondage, or have the slave taught massage or taught to give a pedicure all of which might be more difficult closer to home. The slave should also expect to attend Mistress when She wants to go shopping. he is there to serve Her in any way She desires.

With so much time together the slave can concentrate fully on being a slave and will be expected to keep focussed all the time. But with so much time there are risks his concentration may slip; then he may need punishing.

If the slave needs to fly he will need to take off any metallic items to go through security but can put them on again afterwards. Toys may be inspected as they go through as well but most things will be OK in a suitcase. So Mistress and slave can go off on "holiday" together and both have a good time with the Mistress being pampered and the slave serving.

i have been lucky to be able to travel from time to time with Mistress and to have wonderful times away serving Her. She has used me for learning rope bondage, trained me in massage, and taken me to a spanking party all of which would be impossible nearer to home. But it is the time with Her that is the most important of all.

(See also: bondage, flogging, rope, spanking, dungeon, training)

T is for topping from the bottom

A top is a dominant and a bottom is the submissive who is controlled by the dominant. So topping from the bottom is the activity where the slave tries to control what the Mistress does. It is an inferior trying to manipulate their superior and it is wrong.

A slave may have ideas of what might be a good idea to use for the next time he is able to be with his Mistress. he might beg for a good flogging or to be put into a particular type of bondage. Mistress and slave might relax talking about options for future sessions or about what went particular well in a previous session and was enjoyed by both.

There is nothing wrong with this and a Mistress will want to know how Her slave felt when specific things were being done to him. She will need to know if there were any problems or ones that might arise. If he might be exposed if he went home after a session bruised and marked or with painted toe nails She needs to know. Communication between slave and Mistress is essential to the development of their association and his development as a slave.

But when he is trying to manipulate her to get out of things he finds hard but She wants to do or to do things She does not want to do then it all changes. he is the slave and She should be the one making the decisions. She must be totally free to decide and not be under pressure from her slave. he is abusing Her and this should not be allowed. A slave who persistently tops from the bottom is not an asset to a Mistress but a nuisance and in some cases this can lead to him being dismissed. In other situations he will need to be reminded if he steps across the line to push his own agenda. If he does it again he will be punished severely.

(See also: domination, submission, training)

T is for Torment and torture

Mistresses torment and torture their slaves in many different ways but it is always consensual. Torture is usually seen as what happens when police and military from various regimes torture suspects to get information out of them or prisoners to show their power. It is illegal in International Law but it still goes on all the time. Even countries like the US and the UK usually seen as law abiding have been implicated in the torture of subjects either directly as at "Abu Graib" in Iraq or by handing people over to other regimes who they know are going to torture them.

Torment and torture in BDSM are different. It may be painful, humiliating and uncomfortable but the intention is not to harm even if it is to inflict pain. Both the Mistress and the slave know what is going on. There are safe words to allow things to stop or slow down, and the whole aim is to be safe, sane, and consensual.

The intensity of the torment may be mild or become more severe but the intention is not to produce lasting harm. If this is the case UK law says no one can consent to it and so it is assault. This is the line taken in the UK about branding though other countries see things differently.

But even if there are things a Mistress cannot do there is so much She can do to Her slave. He has a penis and balls which can be crushed, flogged and treated to hot wax, ice, or heating creams until they feel on fire. The balls can be crushed under the Mistress's heel, twisted or made to carry heavy weights. This is all termed CBT for cock and ball torment and can also include the use of electric shocks to this sensitive area.

The nipples are very sensitive and can be clamped, pulled, twisted and crushed with weights hung on them and hot wax dripped on as well. A gagged slave can be beaten and paddled and caned until he cries out in agony. He can be placed into positions that are uncomfortable and kept there, or heated up in a rubber bag or frozen in a bath of cold water. Many of these torments can be applied simultaneously with bondage, torment to the cock and balls and a flogging or caning all at the same time. They can go on for hours together or one after another until the slave is worn down.

So many ways to torment and torture a slave but Mistress will decide which of them to use and how severely. The slave is there to take it and to suffer as Mistress and he have agreed.

(See also, bondage, branding, caning, CBT, consent, electrics, heating cream, ice, nipples, nettles, submission, training, wax)

U is for Uncertainty

One of the most amazing things about being a slave is that there is always uncertainty in what is going to happen next. There may have been discussion between Mistress and slave of what might happen but that does not mean the slave will know it will occur. The slave may have begged to try something new but he will not know if Mistress has decided on it as well

So every day there is a mixture of certainty and uncertainty. The slave knows what his training regime requires him to do including what he shall wear, including collar and chastity, what food to eat and the exercises he must do but at any moment he may receive a text or email ordering him to change what he is doing, to do something else or perform extra tasks for Mistress. He lives his life checking email and texts for today's orders though nothing may come for days or weeks things could all change in an instant if Mistress wants it.

When he attends Mistress he knows he must go to his knees and prostrate himself before Her but what is going to happen next. He may think he knows but Mistress might change Her mind.

So he must learn to cope with uncertainty, the uncertainty that comes from knowing that Mistress is in control and will use Her power

Things are even more uncertain for slaves who are to be punished. Some punishments may be known in advance and declared when he was sentenced by Mistress sitting in Judgement on him. But She may also have set up other punishments that She knows what they are but slave is not told.

He may know he is to be flogged or caned but not how severe it might be or for how long. He will have been worrying and apprehensive since Mistress made Her judgement. This is all deliberate as Mistress wants him to suffer the uncertainty of his fate with its worry and fear of what is to come. She will decide and he will not know until it happens

(See also: domination, judgement, power, punishment, submission, training)

U is for Uniform

Mistress may want Her slaves to be dressed in Her uniform. This may be a simple livery of tea shirt and slacks or something more complex. Mistress has a uniform for me with a tea shirt with embossed on it my slave registration number, track suit bottoms, black shoes or plimsoles and a jacket with Her logo on the back.

That is how She likes me to dress when we are out together with a lead threaded down the left arm so She can grab it if She wants to.

This is a simple livery. Her livery. Her uniform for slaves. Other Mistresses may like something more extreme. Slaves may be kept naked except for their collar and chastity and chains. They may be forced to wear female attire, tights, pants or a thong and a bra to look ridiculous. They may be expected to dress entirely in female clothes or as a "French Maid".

Uniform is there to take away identity and emphasise the fact that Mistress is in control. She will decide what a slave will wear in Her service. It is not for the slave to suggest a uniform though She may make him go and obtain one. He will find it difficult to be sent out to buy female pants or a tong for himself or to go out to get a waitress uniform or something more embarrassing.

Uniform is what Mistress wants her slave to wear. This is not an option but an order and he must obey Her.

(See also: forced feminization, humiliation, ownership, sissy, training)

U is for Urine

Mistress like all people produces urine. The golden liquid She passes is Hers so what She does with it is Her business.

But sometimes Mistresses likes to make their slaves drink urine either that of the slave or that of the Mistress. This is safe as the urine is sterile and will not spread infection but it may not necessarily taste all that nice especially if Mistress or slave have been eating asparagus or other foods which change its taste and smell.

If Mistress wants Her slave to drink urine he must obey. But he may find it difficult at first though the taste may not be bad like some of the other things that Mistress may require him to drink or eat. If presented with a glass of Mistress's urine to drink he should thank Her, drink it down then thank Her again. She is sharing something of Herself with him and he should be pleased to receive it.

But it may not be so easy for him for Mistress may want to use him as Her toilet. There are toilet boxes into which his head can be placed with a toilet seat for Mistress to sit upon, but She may want just to squat down and use him directly with the urine pouring into his mouth so he has to swallow fast to keep up with the flow. If Mistress wants to use the slave in any way at all and he consents then this is always possible. This is the context of his being used as a toilet. No more than a piece of furniture like the footstool, hat stand, candle holder or seat that he may be used for at other times. And there are other things that Mistress 's personal waste disposal unit can be expected to accept and swallow including Her bath water, kitchen scraps, washing up water or anything else She decides needs to be flushed away down into a slave.
(See also: ashtray, domination, furniture, ownership, power, submission)

V is for violation of orders

If a slave is given an order he must obey it. If He has agreed to carry out training outside of sessions with his Mistress than this is expected unless something major prevents it. A slave with a broken leg may not be able to do all his exercises or wear the tights his Mistress has ordered.

But if the slave cannot carry out an order then he must tell his Mistress. If She accepts his reasons he will be OK. If She rejects his reasons and repeats the order he must comply.

Failure to carry out orders either between attendances or in a session is a failure to consider his Mistress. It will be seen as a failure of the slave's obedience and will be punished.

If the order was clear such as not to communicate with or visit a professional dominant has been disregarded then the punishment may be that he is dismissed with no appeal. Mistress will decide. She has the power to dismiss him or bar him from her presence.

Not all crimes are as much a "capital punishment crime" as this. There are often circumstances where a punishment will act to remind him forcibly of his failure and prevent it happening again. Then it is retribution for his crime but transforming in that it prevents it happening again.

For the slave, of course, the punishment may be severe or light depending on what Mistress feels is right. It will not be something he likes done to him. It could be a severe caning or flogging much more severe than anything he has ever suffered before but it could be anything else Mistress thinks fits the bill and the crime.

No doubt at all. Violation of orders shows a lack of respect for Mistress. There is no defence and only future obedience will work to get the slave back into Mistress's good books.

(See also: cane, contracts, punishment, training)

V is for vibrators

There are many devices of all shapes and sizes that vibrate. Some are large and used for loosening stiff muscles by Physiotherapists and others for more intimate contact and vibration to lead to pleasure and orgasm.

The slave is controlled by Mistress and may be helpless in bondage. A vibrator can be applied to any part of his body. It may be pleasant and arousing but he has no control over it. He may be hooded or blindfolded so he has no idea of what is coming.

A slave subjected to a vibrator on his nipples, penis or balls or thrust deeply inside his anus is the plaything of his Mistress.

She will decide the rhythm and the intensity and a vibrator that is set on a high setting and applied to a tender area will give pain to the slave not pleasure.

So Mistress decides if it is to be pain or pleasure, and also where and when, just like all the other devices She uses to control and torment Her slaves.

For a Mistress who is the partner of her slave the sight of the Mistress pleasuring herself whilst the slave is unable to move, helpless and unable to reach an orgasm himself from his chastity can be very arousing. She has the pleasure and he has the discomfort as his penis is constrained and he cannot even touch his Mistress whilst She enjoys Herself. Perfect!

(See also: darkness and disorientation, sensation and stimulation, sex)

V is for Violet Wand

A violet wand is used to produce a static electrical charge from the AC current from the mains and to charge a hollow glass electrode which can be placed on the skin and discharge itself through a spark. The energy level is extremely low. It is identical to the static charge you can get from rubbing a glass surface with a cloth and which goes to your finger giving a slight shock.

The charge goes to the surface of the skin and does not penetrate deeper but it can activate the nerves in the skin. If mild it gives a buzzing sensation but if the power is higher then it is painful. But it looks spectacular as the spark goes from the glass electrode to the skin with a spark joining the two. There is no risk of the electrocution which can come from AC power from the mains.

So the slave lies there or kneels or stands as Mistress has decided and sparks come form the device to earth themselves on his nipples, his penis, his balls, or any part of his skin. Unlike any other electrical device it is safe to use the violet wand above the waist.

A slave who is to be shocked with a violet wand feels vulnerable as Mistress holds in Her hand the electrode which will shock him.

(See also: electrics, shock collar, zapped)

V is for Vulnerable

When a slave hands himself over voluntarily to his Mistress he makes himself vulnerable. He is placed in bondage from which he cannot escape and Mistress can do with him what She wants.

Although he puts himself at risk he does so in a situation where he has agreed it and has trust that his Mistress will keep him safe. But there are always risks in what Mistress and slave do. He may end up with marks difficult to explain at home if She did not realise that he could not be marked, rope burns if rope is too tight or taken off too quickly or other damage. Good communication to decide what is possible is essential and being slave to a Mistress and attending Her regularly means that communication and trust both are built up so that there is a real relationship between Mistress and slave.

His vulnerability to Mistress is such an arousing thing. He is helpless and She is squeezing his nipples, crushing his balls, shocking him with the electrics and flogging him and there is nothing he can do about it (except for a safe word). i find that the feeling of vulnerability excites me both with the bondage and all Mistress does to me and this is very arousing indeed. Of course physically i am also constrained by the steel tube of my chastity device so becoming aroused just leads to even more discomfort.

Physical vulnerability is one element but as a slave i open myself up to Mistress and make myself psychologically vulnerable as well. She really does know both me and all my secrets. So if She was to decide to tell others, put it all on "Facebook" or anything else i would be devastated. But i trust her and She ensures that i do not get carried away getting confused between my roles at work, home and as Her slave. She protects me against myself. In many ways the psychological vulnerability is greater than the physical situation as there are limits to the physical situation and it can be stopped with the use of a safe word but none to what is happening in my brain.

We all have a past with experiences back even to childhood that were nice and some that were disturbing. Many slaves have hidden such negative memories for years even decades and when they begin to explore the world of submission there are risks. It is so exciting that it is easy to forget everything else in the moment. So many slaves who have hidden their submissive nature but also have other issues. They may have suffered physical, mental or even sexual abuse and locked it all away at the bottom of their mind.

Entering the state of being a slave, even in a short session, can unlock these memories or those horrors so there is a real risk that the distress caused can just spill out suddenly. The slave is being watched by Mistress who will not let him be harmed but She may not know what is going on inside.

So She watches closely for distress disproportionate to what is going on. Even if the slave does not use his safe word She is prepared to stop to support and to let him talk about it.

i have found that the support Mistress gives me , her open style of communication and the fact that i can be fully open with her not just on my desire for submission but on all sorts of other things has been a tremendous help with difficult things. She has been to some extent both my Mistress and my psychotherapist, though with an unusual style of psychotherapy approach. This has allowed me to expose my most inmost being, my past, my fears, everything.

This comes at a cost. There is the slave feeling wrung out both physically and emotionally after a session, often termed a "drop". Then Mistress supports, chats, provides cups of tea and helps me regain equilibrium. But there is also a cost to Her.

Many Mistresses have had their own issues as well and these may surface in the Mistress mind during the session. By supporting the slave She is making Herself vulnerable not least to her own internal strains. Slaves need to be considerate to Mistress's needs and issues as well as their own. She may be having an "off" day, have pain from a physical or psychological cause and show Her distress in session. If Mistress stops something because She needs to that is all OK. She is in change and Her needs come first. But a slave needs to learn to be considerate of Mistress in all Her aspects. He does not need to know why there is a problem unless She chooses to share with him but he need to realise that by taking charge She is making herself vulnerable as well and She must also not come to any harm.

(See also: consent, domination, submission, training)

W is for Wall

Naughty children are told to face the wall or to stand in the corner. Slaves may be made to stand up against the wall or in the corner too. Whether a slave has done anything wrong or not Mistress can make him stand where She wants and this includes facing the wall, standing on tiptoe, or facing a corner and remaining standing for hours. He has been told to keep still so this is what he must do and he does not know if Mistress is there just behind him watching or not.

Mistress may not have access to a dungeon with all the facilities that it contains but her rooms do have walls and they can be used to secure a slave. If She wants to be able to tether him on his knees for long periods a ringbolt on the lower part of the wall will act as a place to attach the chains and lock them securely.

If She wants him spread eagled against the wall four ring bolts will mean She can have him secured with his legs apart and his arms above his head, ready for flogging. Or She can just leave him attached like that and the cramps will develop after he has been standing for a while.

If there is a small alcove it can be turned into a cage or place he can be attached for sleeping at night.

Walls give us all security but for the slave Mistress may want to use them to imprison him and keep him chained up and secure in a different sense.

(See also, cage, cupboard, wheel)

W is for water torture

Waterboarding was used by the Japanese first then the US military as an interrogation aid. It involves covering the face of the victim and then pouring on water until he is nearly drowning. It is a torture and nothing less so rarely used by Mistresses on their slaves.

But water can be used to torment slaves in other ways as well. If the slave is placed in a cold bath and kept there he will get colder and colder, even more if his bath has been filled with ice.

If he is made to stand outside in the rain naked or to remain in wet clothes he will soon be shivering uncontrollably.

A slave can be made to drink large quantities of water but not allowed to go to pass urine. he will gradually fill up his bladder until he feels he is about to burst or has to wet himself. This is humiliating as he begs to be allowed to wee but cannot do it until Mistress agrees.

If Mistress has a wet room She can keep the slave hooded and in the dark and stimulate him with the shower, ice cold, hot, directly onto his private parts or his face and he will have no idea of what is coming next. If there is space outside a hosepipe can be used to spray the slave. High flows from a pressure washer hurt and can cause bruises and show who is the boss. The major risk of using water is that everything else including the Mistress get wet as well.

(See also: humiliation, ice, torment and torture,)

W is for Wheel

One way to secure and torment slaves is to place them on "The Wheel". This secures them with legs opened and arms out with multiple straps holding legs, arms and body in place. The wheel is attached to a wall and can be rotated so they may be upright or upside down. Attached facing the wheel they are well placed for flogging. Facing out all the tender parts, nipples, cock and balls are all available to torture.

But this is a very expensive piece of equipment costing thousands of dollars and needs careful installation. It is not something that can be easily hidden or packed away. A wheel is sometimes the centre piece of commercial dungeon and it looks very impressive.

So to access time on the wheel you need to find a chamber with one, make sure you have some time and the slave is secured so he cannot fall off and then Mistress can have fun. It is equipment to travel to or to seek from a professional and commercial dungeon in most cases. But the feeling of vulnerability as secured to the wheel it is rotated and a slave does not know whether he will be upside down or upright next is most exciting.

(See also: whipping bench, cage, rack)

W is for weights

A slave can be expected to lose weight or to stay at an ideal weight decided by Mistress. She may impose food restriction with exercise regimes. She does not want a fat, flabby slave but one who is slim and toned to Her specifications.

Weights can be added to bondage to make things difficult for the slave. He may be made to carry heavy weights up and down stairs until he is exhausted, particularly if he is made to do the exercise in chains or manacles. He can be required to move 1000 Kg of soil or rocks from one part of the garden to another and then back again. He can be put to "hard labour".

Weights hung from the balls stretch them and drag them down. 1-2 kg of weights hanging there makes it difficult for the slave to walk and is very uncomfortable, especially if they are suspended from a parachute ball stretcher filled with sharp pointed pins. But weights can also be a heavy steel ring attached around the balls separate from the penis and worn without supporting underpants. The balls hang down all day and the slave will not forget he is wearing it. Weights can also be hung from his nipple clamps. They stretch the nipples and the clamps fell even tighter and can be made to swing back and forth like a pendulum.

Mistress can take time adding ever greater weights to his parts until the slave is in agony. It looks a funny sight to see a slave with his legs held apart and with a bag of weights swinging to and fro. For fun Mistress could play a weight forfeit game. She hangs a bag on his balls and then asks general knowledge questions. Each time he gets one wrong She adds another weight. This can also be done with a bucket instead and glasses of water added each time until the bucket is full and the slave so distracted by the pain that he will not be able to answer even the simplest question.

Of course the questions do not need to be simple at all as the object is for the slave to fail to give the right answer and to get more weights added.

Mistress has used 1kg weights on each nipple and up to 5lb (2.5Kg) weights hanging on my balls or had me pull along a heavier weight attached to cock and balls together.

(See also: bondage, CBT, nipples)

W is for work

A slave may have a life of slavery alone but most have a life in work as well. Whatever their work they probably need to keep their slavery hidden but that does not mean that servitude stops when they reach the office.

A slave can be required to wear collar, nipple clamps, ankle chains and chastity, with or without women's pants or a thong, bra, constrictive clothing or even a corset under his outside clothing. he can be expected to find a quiet place in the car park to eat his cat food for lunch or ordered never to use the stairs even if he works in a 12 storey office block. All of this is kept hidden and keeps the slave on his toes. Text messages and private emails can alert the slave to what he must do after work or get on the way home. Mistress is still in control where it matters. And of course he is in chastity at work whilst She has the only key.

Work for Mistress is equally important if not more so. A slave will have his domestic services to perform and those personal services Mistress requires. This may mean he needs to get up one or two hours early to get the tasks completed before going to work. She will always have jobs for him to do.

So the slave may be always at work part for his employer and all of the time for Mistress and he needs are the most important. She comes first.

He may be put to "hard labour" either for tasks that need doing gardening, moving stuff or cleaning but also for tasks of no value at all decided by Mistress, moving piles of soil or stones and then taking them back to where they came from or digging a deep hole and then filling it in. These are tasks designed to work him hard and show that he is obedient even when it becomes difficult. Any slacking will be punished severely.

All the time at work he bondage is there but hidden but away from work it can be done in chains, heavy collar an manacles, dressed , uniformed, or naked as Mistress desires. Slaves work for Mistress full time. This is how it should be.

(See also: chains, corsets, domestic service, manacles, ownership, personal services,)

W is for Wax

Wax can be used to remove hair with soft wax in strips to pull off body hair and hard wax to remove all the hair from the private parts. Mistress requires me to have my nipples waxed and a regular Brazilian wax down below but allows me to keep other hair. Other Mistresses require wax removal of all hair regularly and a shaving of the head as well.

Hot wax can also be used to stimulate and torment a slave. First make sure that the wax is not so hot it will burn and choose candles or paraffin wax with a low melting point. Then the wax can be dripped upon all parts of the slave when he is restrained, helpless and blindfolded.

As the wax hits the tip of the penis, the balls or the nipples there is immediate pain followed by a feeling of heat. The wax cools and sets and can either be left in placed or scraped off to allow more to be applied. All you need is a lighted candle or tea light and a prepared slave.

i find it feels really hot and shocks me as the wax hits the skin but then as it solidifies it feels good as the feeling of being boiled recedes until the next drop hits. It feels good and allows Mistress to be creative with wax of different colours and patterns on my body.

But She can also apply large amounts of wax. i can be made to dip my nipples in a bowl of liquid wax and hold them there until it sets. My cock and balls can be dipped alternating between ice/water and liquid wax. This leads to a build up of wax layer on layer with alternating heat and cold. It is difficult to lie with your parts in a bowl of ice and water or hot wax whilst Mistress counts the seconds until you can get up and plunge in the other material. Over time the layers cover the penis and balls and it turns into a solid block of hard wax; A heavy block which hangs down and swings to and fro as i move. Of course a slave so encased cannot pass urine and must expect to suffer discomfort from not being able to do so if kept like this for hours.

Wax prepares the slave as Mistress wishes him to look and used carefully allows Her to enjoy Herself tormenting the slave and making things difficult for him as well.

(See also: Brazilian wax, CBT, heating cream, ice, nipples)

W is for Whip

A Mistress who wants to strike Her slave has many ways to do it. She may use her hand to spank him. She might consider a paddle, the sole of her trainers, or a tawse or her crop. Multiple tail whips are termed floggers and they can be used to run over the skin softly which is definitely a sensuous feeling or down onto the skin with a real bite, knocking the breath out of the slave , sharp and hard at the same time.

Whips expand the range of equipment that a Mistress can use. Someone who is into horse riding may use a short whip to help control their mount or a long whip with a flexible end if driving a carriage pulled by horses. These implements can be obtained from riding suppliers and used on slaves. There is a sharp crack as the whip is brought down and it feels like there is a line of fire along the skin where the whip has struck. These whips are also useful for guiding and chastising slaves who are functioning as ponies, pulling a cart or being ridden by a Mistress. They may be long or short but they allow accurate placement of the tip which causes the pain.

These whips tend to be thin and flexible and cause a sting on the skin. Thicker whips with one long tail have much more energy where they hit and they will hurt a lot more. There is a risk that the tip of the whip may wrap around the body giving out most of that energy elsewhere from the site desired and the "wrapping" may cause damage, bruising or break the skin

Whips need to be kept clean, flexible and sometimes require oiling to make them easier to use. They really hurt and repeated strokes over a backside or a back may leave the slave bruised, tender, and marked for days. If your slave cannot be marked a heavy whip is not the best item to choose but if it does not matter than it is a powerful weapon in Mistress's armoury. Very severe whipping can strip of the skin, bruise and damage the underlying muscles and even leave the slave permanently marked and scarred.

The use of the long "bullwhip" to crack the whip just above the surface of the skin so it makes a noise but does not touch the target some of the time and arrives with full force on other strokes is an art. It takes practice and may need lessons to show how to get the best out of it. Some Mistresses can use a whip in either hand with two whips at once striking the slave from both sides at the same time.

It is good that Mistress has a range of items that She can decide to use with paddles, spanking, flogging, the crop, cane, horse whip or even whipping with a 6ft bull whip all available to her when She wants them.

(See also: cane, crop, flogger, spanking, tawse)

W is for Whipping bench

A whipping bench is a piece of furniture designed so that the slave lies face down upon it strapped down so he cannot move and it puts his backside up in the air to give the best possible target for Mistress to beat, flog or cane.

A padded whipping bench has the advantage that the backside is at just the right height for whipping and also the slave can be kept in this position for hours waiting for the whipping to begin in the dark and hooded.

They are expensive but well worth the investment. Some can be collapsed so they can be put out sight but others will stand there in the corner of a room reminding the slave of the whipping to come and the Mistress of the opportunity to use the device.

Most commercial dungeons and dungeons for hire have whipping benches so if you have not tried it you can book an appointment and give it a try so the Mistress can enjoy time flogging the slave and the slave receive a very good flogging indeed, all strokes on target.

(See also: cage, flogging, whip, rack, X position)

W is for Whipping slave

In medieval times princes and the aristocracy flogged their children when they were disobedient. Except this was not always the case as the child might have someone allocated to take "their" whipping as their whipping boy.

If Mistress likes flogging or whipping a slave and finds it convenient and relaxing after a day of stress then the slave may be volunteered to be Her whipping slave. It is not that he wants it. It is not that he has done anything wrong to be punished. It is just that Mistress needs someone to use to get irritation out of her system.

So a whipping slave fulfils these needs. He is there to take a whipping when She wants to do it. his service to Mistress is to take the beating and not complain. She works out her irritation and tensions and he is helping Her. This can be an ideal arrangement. But it does not stop her flogging him hard for anything he does wrong as well or just because She feels like it.

(See also: ownership, submission)

X is for X position

Many pictures of slaves being chastised show them shackled to an X shaped frame. This is commonly seen in professional dungeons but not an easy thing to have around the average house.

The advantage of the X position is that the slave is secured with arms spread above his head and legs apart. he cannot put his legs together to protect himself. he is in an ideal position for flogging , nipple play or CBT. he cannot resist. But if he has difficulty moving his arms above his head the position is difficult to maintain.

If Mistress has no space for an X frame an alternative is to have a number of ring bolts on the floor or wall. The slave can be attached to them with legs spread and arms secured. The ring bolts may need to be camouflaged in an average house and hidden behind furniture but it does not take long to have a slave shackled ready for action.

It is all about Mistress being able to place her slaves how She wants them, helpless and ready for anything She wants to do.

(See also: bondage, cage, whipping stool, wall, wheel, rack)

Y is for Yes Mistress

Slaves must be obedient to their Mistress. They have consented to it. They have agreed in their slave contract. They have discussed options of what She will do to them and potentially things She might do as well.

Now this has been agreed the next step is clear. Yes Mistress is the answer they must give to all Her orders. These are orders and not requests and the slave is there to submit and obey Her.

There is always the use of the safe word to stop things if they are al too much but that is something which should be used very rarely.

So Yes Mistress is the answer to ALL the orders from Mistress. Yes Mistress means obedience and that is the basis of all their slavery.

YES Mistress, You have control over Your slave.

(See also: contracts, domination, ownership, submission, safe word)

Z is for Zapped

A slave is zapped by his Mistress to give him an electric shock.

It may be a shock to his balls from his shock collar wrapped around them with Mistress carrying the remote controller in the street and able to zap him from up to 400 yards away.

It could be shocks from the electric box on a lead as he lies there in a heavy hood or blindfold. he does not know whether his penis, balls or anus are going to get shocked , how frequent or how severely.

Mistress might be using a violet wand to make sparks fly from the device to his skin.

His chastity might be fitted with electrics controlled by computer from the other side of the world.

Whatever the system She uses Mistress can zap him any time to keep him focussed on his tasks, to punish failure or even just because She wants to.

(See also; arse, chastity, electrics, remote control, shock collar, training, violet wand)

Z is for Zipper

A zipper is used to close a bondage bag and keep the slave inside. It is always a good idea not to catch his personal parts or his hairs in the zip or he will get severe pain when he is not expecting it and the hairs may cause the zip to jam with him stuck inside the bag or hood.

A zipper is also the term used to describe a number of pegs or clamps on a string. Each is applied to the slave perhaps on the nipples, thighs, penis and balls or the soft skin of the tummy then all are pulled off together, all at once with pain that explodes all over the body as they are removed.

A simple way to give severe pain all over at the same time!

(See also: CBT, clamps, nipples)

Afterwards

We hope you have enjoyed this book and learned more of what it is for a man to become a slave to a powerful Mistress

You may have found much that is new and ideas for your own lives and some things you never expected to see.

Feel free to do anything we have put here but always remember that a male slave consents to all that is done to him, after understanding what it is and that anything less is abuse.

But if he understands and consents and both Mistress and slave want to do something they should get on with it.

However the final decision must always be with Mistress for She should never do anything She does not want to do with her slave.

She is the Mistress and is in control and makes the rules.

Women rule and should do so. **The male is the slave and is there to submit to her will and obey Her. That is what this is all about.**

Mistress's Final Thoughts:

This book tells you the risks of all that you can do to a male slave and where you need to be careful.

But it is such good fun to torment a helpless slave, to lead him into total submission to the will of a powerful Mistress.

It is a way to improve him and bring him to a proper understanding of the place of the male which is at the feet of a Female and lead by Her.

It is possible to train male slaves to perform domestic and personal services allowing the Mistress more time to enjoy herself as She deserves.

Every Woman would benefit from having a male slave.

Enjoy yourselves as the Dominant Mistress as you develop your dominance and the male increases his obedience and submission.

Be safe and sane and consensual and you will have lots and lots of fun if you take this path.

5931523R00185

Printed in Great Britain
by Amazon.co.uk, Ltd.,
Marston Gate.